THE
TAHINI TABLE

THE
TAHINI TABLE

Go Beyond Hummus with 100 Recipes for Every Meal

AMY ZITELMAN

with Andrew Schloss

PHOTOGRAPHY BY Jillian Guyette
FOOD STYLING BY Lisa Russell

A SURREY BOOK

AGATE

CHICAGO

Printed in China

Library of Congress Cataloging-in-Publication Data

Names: Zitelman, Amy, author. | Schloss, Andrew
Title: The tahini table: go beyond hummus with 100 recipes for every meal
   and in between / Amy Zitelman with Andrew Schloss; photography by
   Jillian Guyette.
Description: Chicago: Surrey, 2020. | Includes index. | Summary: "The
   Tahini Table reveals tahini as a versatile, healthy, and delicious
   addition to any kitchen, with more than 100 recipes for snacks, dinners,
   desserts, and more"-- Provided by publisher.
Identifiers: LCCN 2020010226 (print) | LCCN 2020010227 (ebook) | ISBN
   9781572842892 (hardback) | ISBN 9781572848429 (ebook)
Subjects: LCSH: Cooking (Tahini) | LCGFT: Cookbooks.
Classification: LCC TX819.T34 Z57 2020 (print) | LCC TX819.T34 (ebook) |
   DDC 641.5956--dc23
LC record available at https://lccn.loc.gov/2020010226
LC ebook record available at https://lccn.loc.gov/2020010227

10 9 8 7 6 5 4 3 2 1   20 21 22 23 24 25

Art direction and cover design by Morgan Krehbiel
Photography by Jillian Guyette
Food styling by Lisa Russell

Agate books are available in bulk at discount prices.
For more information, visit agatepublishing.com.

DEDICATED TO:

Our grandparents—Bubbe, PopPop Harry,
PopPop Marv, and Grandee

CONTENTS

〜〜〜〜〜〜

FOREWORD

When we met Amy Zitelman at our restaurant Zahav in early 2013, the first question she asked was what brand of tahini we used. We looked at each other, shrugged our shoulders, and said, "Whatever the distributor brings us."

An impromptu blind tasting was arranged on the spot, and we immediately knew we had found our new tahini. We told Amy we'd take whatever was in her car if she could find the loading dock, and the next thing we knew, she was schlepping four 11-pound buckets of Soom tahini through the back door of Zahav. We never even asked about the price, but that was the last time we wouldn't be able to name our tahini brand.

We consider tahini to be the mother sauce of Israeli cuisine, which kind of makes Soom our secret sauce. If you've ever eaten (almost) anything at Zahav, had a bowl of hummus at Dizengoff, or a shake at Goldie, then you're in on the secret. But until Amy and her two sisters came along, we didn't have reliable access to high-quality tahini.

The Zitelmans have done more than anyone to rescue tahini from the dusty back shelves of Middle Eastern groceries and present it to mainstream America as a versatile, healthy, and delicious ingredient. The quality of their tahini is without comparison. But the story of how three sisters took an ancient product and made it new again is even more compelling.

And we have had a front row seat to it all. Like us, Soom is a company born in Philadelphia by way of Israel. This gives us a lot of *nachas*. But that's not why we're saying all these nice things (although it doesn't hurt). We now live in a world where "whatever the distributor brings us" isn't good enough anymore, and we owe a lot of that to the Soom sisters.

The pages that follow contain a head-spinning array of old, new, and inspired uses for tahini, many of which we will be stealing. We live in a moment in time when a renewed appreciation of ancient foodways and culinary traditions intersects with a growing desire to eat naturally, healthfully, and without compromise. It is a moment that is tailor-made for tahini and the perfect time for this book. It's also good timing for us personally; we literally just ran out of ideas for using tahini.

—MICHAEL SOLOMONOV AND STEVEN COOK

INTRODUCTION

~~~~~~~~~~~~~~~~~~~~~~~~~~~~

///**A**re you familiar with tahini?" I must have asked that question thousands of times since we started Soom Foods. In 2011 none of us were thinking much about tahini, but my sister Shelby had a business degree, my other sister Jackie was dating Omri, a tahini expert in Israel, and I needed a job.

One Shabbat, Shelby went to Omri's for dinner. Rachella, Omri's mom, had baked a carrot cake made with tahini instead of oil. Wheels started turning. Tahini in a cake? How can that be? What exactly is this stuff? Why is it so much better than anything we have in the United States? And then Shelby called me with a question that would change all our lives: Could we sell tahini back home where hardly anyone had even heard of it?

In 2013, when we started Soom, I was in a farmers' market or grocery store every day handing out samples. "Are you familiar with tahini?" Other than the people who thought I had said "Tahiti," maybe one in twenty told me they had a can in the fridge that they used only to make hummus. Hummus was a starting point, but as Rachella's cake proved, the culinary potential for really good tahini went way past hummus.

The secret of great tahini is in the seed. Omri imports only Humera sesame seeds from Ethiopia (see page 6). The very best tahini, what we call premium tahini, is made from 100 percent Humera sesame. That is how we make Soom tahini (*soom soom* is Hebrew for sesame). It is why our tahini was different at the time than the others you

1

could get in the United States. Unlike the cans of congealed tahini paste wasting away in the back of countless refrigerators or gathering dust on the bottom shelf of the international aisle, Soom is delicious all by itself and super versatile—an inspiring replacement for the eggs, cheese, mayo, and cream called for in recipes that American home cooks make for their families every day.

From the very beginning, we founded Soom Foods with a vision that tahini would be a staple pantry item in the American market simply because it is a delicious, nutritious, and versatile ingredient. Although this ambition was somewhat far-fetched at the time, tahini is increasingly recognized as a superfood that is rich in omega-6 fatty acids, protein, and calcium. Our sales in the US market have been steady. In 2016 tahini was named "cult condiment" of the year by the Kitchn website. At that time, we were thrilled to be called a condiment—the same food category as established cooking staples like mustard and mayo. And last year Soom was named Best Tahini by *New York* magazine's "The Strategist." We knew a tahini cookbook built around tahini's versatility and potential central role in everyday cooking was a natural next step.

Since we founded Soom, tahini has started to find its place in the mainstream of American cooking. It's already changed the way my family eats and the way I cook, and in the following pages you will discover scores of recipes that show how bringing tahini to your table can do the same for you.

A Word About *I* and *We*: I accomplish nothing of consequence alone, which is why I have a hard time talking about myself and my opinions as if they were just mine. At Soom, everything (well, maybe not *everything*) is a team decision, a team activity, or a team project. Same thing at home, or working on this book. When I'm talking about something personal, I will say "I," but when it's something that matters, something that I know is true and important, I'm going to say "we," because that's who deserves the credit.

CHAPTER 1

YOUR TAHINI KITCHEN

Tahini is a paste that is made with nothing more than roasted and pressed sesame seeds. Sesame seeds are an ancient food—there's evidence that they have been cultivated in India since 5000 BCE! Tahini itself is also old, having been listed as an ingredient in a hummus recipe in an Egyptian cookbook from the thirteenth century. Today, tahini has spread across the globe, probably because it is so delicious, nutritious, and, as you'll see, versatile.

Because premium tahini is so pure and simple, it makes itself at home in any cuisine that uses sesame. This includes most of the cooking traditions of the Eastern Mediterranean, plus all of North Africa, the Stans (Kazakhstan, Tajikistan, Uzbekistan, Turkmenistan, Afghanistan, and Pakistan), the entirety of South Asia (India, Burma, Cambodia, Thailand, Laos, and Vietnam), and all of the far Eastern Asian cuisines. Though its historical roots are in the Middle East, we see tahini as an all-purpose ingredient that can be a stir-fry sauce, a drizzle for curries, or a dressing for a noodle bowl. It is also mild enough to step in as a substitute in recipes that call for eggs, oil, and more, which is great for those with dietary restrictions and sensitivities.

Premium tahini is creamy and tastes light yet rich, nutty, and savory—the kind of thing you wouldn't mind eating from the jar. It's packed full of vitamins A and E, calcium, magnesium, and iron. And because of its high healthy fat content, tahini can easily replace sometimes troublesome ingredients such as butter, eggs, and cream in many recipes. What's not to love? In this chapter, we'll cover the tahini basics and a few other details that will help you set up your tahini kitchen.

TAHINI BASICS

Tahini has only one ingredient: sesame seeds, roasted and ground. If the label on a jar of tahini lists more than one ingredient, put it down and walk away. But even that doesn't guarantee that a tahini is premium. To be premium, the type of sesame seeds makes a difference.

The world's most highly prized sesame seeds come from Ethiopia, from the rich soil around Humera, a town in the Tigray region on the border of Eritrea and Sudan. Of the dozens of sesame varieties grown in Asia and Africa, the Humera variety is the only one described consistently as buttery, and it is regarded throughout the world as the definitive variety for tahini. Most of the worldwide production of sesame is used for oil, but not Humera seeds, which are reserved exclusively for tahini. When we refer to premium tahini in this book, we mean tahini that's made from 100 percent Humera sesame seeds—and nothing else.

Sesame seeds grow in multichambered pods, about two dozen pods per plant. When ripe, the pods turn from bright green to reddish tan, and they pop open along the seams where one chamber meets another, revealing hundreds of pearly white seeds, each one protected by a hard shell. Before roasting, the shells are cracked off and the seeds are gently roasted in a double-walled steam oven until they burnish to a uniform golden color. Toasting brings out the nutty flavor of the sesame, but also some bitterness. It is important to keep the sesame seeds from toasting too dark or they become too bitter to grind into tahini.

***Tahini* or *tehina*?** They're different spellings of the same word that reflect the difference in pronunciation between Greek and Arabic—"i" for Greek and "a" for Arabic (and Hebrew). Even though our experience with tahini is Israeli, at Soom (and in this book) we use the Greek spelling because it is more common in the United States.

OIL ON TOP

SHAKEN

STIRRED

USING AND STORING TAHINI

When sesame seeds are ground, their fiber and protein are pulverized, and the oil they once held in suspension flows out. When tahini is initially manufactured, the mixture is smooth and cohesive, with nothing but a few shimmers of oil peeking through its matte surface. As the tahini sits in the jar, the ground-up solid part sinks to the bottom and the fluid oil gathers on the surface. The same thing happens to any all-natural 100 percent seed or nut butter; seed and nut butters that *don't* separate in the jar have added saturated fat, usually in the form of palm oil or hydrogenated vegetable oil, which keeps them creamy.

Tahini made from low-quality seeds can have a large amount of oil floating on the top, almost half its volume. Low-quality tahini also tends to have a bitter, astringent quality that can make your tongue feel dry and chalky. If this has been your experience in the past, I encourage you to seek out the good stuff! Premium tahini made from Humera sesame seeds is nothing like that.

When you open a new jar of premium tahini, the oil sitting on top will be no deeper than an inch, and the sesame paste underneath will still be fluid enough to insert a stirrer without resistance. At the bottom of the jar, your stirrer may hit a thin layer of firm sesame paste, especially as you stir into the corners of the jar. To combine everything before using, simply shake the jar vigorously. At first you will hear the oil splashing, but soon the splashing sound will become more like a "glug." That sound change indicates that the oil and fluid paste have combined. Then open the lid, peel off the seal, and dig in with a long-handled fork to scrape up any firm stuff from the bottom. Use your finger to push it off the fork and back into the jar, and in one or two more stirs, all of the tahini in the jar will be completely creamy.

You can store opened jars of tahini in or out of the refrigerator, and they'll keep for a good long time—Soom tahini is usable for up to two years from its production date. Over time all tahini will separate, but cold helps keep the oil in suspension longer. Storing it at room temperature ensures that your tahini will stay pourable, which is what I prefer.

TAHINI SAUCE

Tahini in the jar or can is technically tahini paste. It is a cooking ingredient and not typically eaten by itself. When tahini paste is mixed with lemon juice, salt, garlic, and often cumin, and thinned with cold water, it becomes tahini sauce. Tahini sauce is served everywhere in Arabic cooking. It is the topping for falafel and shawarma, and one of the two main ingredients in hummus.

When turning tahini paste into tahini sauce, you have to thin it out so that it flows. But there's a problem: As soon as tahini paste touches water, lemon juice, or anything containing water, it turns grainy and stiff, just the opposite of creamy and smooth. This happens every time you make tahini sauce, so when it clumps, don't freak. All you have to do is add cold water, a few tablespoons at a time, and whisk vigorously. At a certain point, all of a sudden, your sauce will switch from grainy gunk the color of wet sand into a beautifully pale emulsion the consistency of softly beaten cream.

Unlike tahini paste, tahini sauce has to be refrigerated, because the added water makes the sauce perishable. When you make one of our delicious tahini sauce recipes in chapter 2, don't make more than you can use in a few days. We have found that storing tahini sauce in glass containers is better than plastic. Tahini is sort of sticky, and scrubbing it off plastic is a chore. Glass cleans up way faster.

We know lots of professional chefs who use a food processor when they make tahini sauce. That's because they are cooking in volume. Since you'll be making only enough sauce for two or three days, it makes a lot more sense to use a mixing bowl and a whisk. It's fast, and cleanup is so much easier.

HUMMUS BI TAHINI AND CHICKPEAS

Hummus (pronounced HOO-moos—to be authentic make a vibration in the back of your throat as you sound the "h") is Arabic for "chickpeas." The chickpea spread made from cooked chickpeas and tahini sauce that Americans (and this book) call "hummus" is known as "hummus bi tahini" in the Middle East.

Cultivated chickpeas have been found in the Middle East in archeological digs that date to around 3500 BCE. There is no other ingredient that has deeper roots in the food of the ancient Eastern Mediterranean. They are nutritionally dense, providing more than 20 percent of the daily value of protein, dietary fiber, folate, iron, and phosphorus. Soaked dried chickpeas that you cook yourself and canned chickpeas that are cooked in a factory have similar nutritional profiles, and both can be used to make good hummus. The largest difference is texture.

Dried chickpeas can be cooked to maintain their shape or cooked to a mush, which is preferable for hummus. Canned chickpeas are manufactured to maintain their shape, so hummus made from canned chickpeas will not be as creamy as hummus made from homecooked chickpeas. But if you cook drained canned chickpeas, covered with water and a pinch of baking soda,

SOAKED

DRIED

COOKED TO
MAINTAIN SHAPE

COOKED TO MUSH

they'll turn to mush in about 15 minutes. Baking soda's natural alkalinity helps the fibers in the chickpeas dissolve, which will result in hummus of unsurpassed creaminess.

You'll find several recipes for different kinds of hummus in this book, and hummus, in turn, is used as a component in many more.

CHOCOLATE TAHINI AND HALVAH

Several recipes call for chocolate tahini, a confection spread made from tahini, sugar, and cocoa. It can be used as a sweet spread on cookies, cakes, or bread, or as an ingredient in baking and candy making. At Soom we sell chocolate sweet tahini. When a recipe in the book calls for chocolate tahini, that is the product we used for development. Chocolate tahini is not much different from chocolate nut butters, and the products can pretty much be used interchangeably.

Made from tahini and sugar, halvah is the most common confection in the Middle East. It is usually dense and either slightly gelatinous or crumbly, depending on how it's made. In this book, we include recipes for making halvah from tahini, and we use halvah, store-bought or homemade, as an ingredient in other recipes.

OTHER COMMON INGREDIENTS

Now that we've told you more than you probably need to know about tahini and chickpeas, there are a few other ingredients we use all the time that also have great stories. As Andy and I worked on this book, it seems that he knew trivia about every ingredient I picked up. He showed me that knowing where an ingredient comes from and how it behaves can inspire us to use it with more creativity. If there are ingredients you aren't familiar with, don't worry, as they will become pantry staples soon enough. For more information on our favorite brands and tools, see the Resources section on page 230.

AVOCADOS

Thick-skinned and creamy fleshed, the semitropical avocado is one of two fruits that ripen only after they are picked (the other is the banana). So, the best place to store avocados to keep them from overripening is on the tree. Once they are harvested, they will ripen in about a week.

All commercially grown avocados are hybrids, derived from three geographical varieties: Mexican avocados are small and high in fat; lowland Guatemalan avocados are large, with coarse, watery flesh; and highland Guatemalan avocados are pale green and have moderate fat and small pits. Most avocados sold in the United States are Hass avocados from California, a hybrid of the Mexican fruit, with rough, dark hides and a rich, creamy flesh. The remainder are mostly Fuerte and Booth, both Guatemalan hybrids, and grow mostly in Florida. They are large, smooth skinned, and bright green. Their flesh is mealier than Hass and lower in fat.

As with many tropical and subtropical fruit, an avocado's ripening cycle is enhanced by warm temperature and stopped by cold. Avocados ripen best between 65°F and 75°F, and their cellular machinery grinds to a halt when temperatures drop below 45°F. Ripe avocados can be refrigerated for several days without damage.

Because they contain enzymes that encourage oxidation, avocados are prone to browning from exposure to air. You can stop the degradation by rubbing the cut flesh with citrus juice, which interrupts the enzyme action. Coating the surface with oil or placing plastic wrap right against the avocado's surface work because they keep air away.

CITRUS JUICE AND ZEST

Tahini and citrus are flavor-mates— lemon juice especially. You can't make tahini sauce without it. The flavor of freshly squeezed citrus juice is always

better than bottled, which is why we specify it in our recipes, but when a recipe calls for a lot of juice, freshly squeezed can sometimes be prohibitively expensive. There are a few brands of bottled juice that taste pretty good; the one we like best is Santa Cruz.

One advantage of fresh over bottled juice is that fresh citrus all come covered in aromatic zest, the colorful part of the peel that is loaded with citrus oil. Zest gives you the flavor of citrus without any acid, helpful when you want to add citrusy flavor to fresh dairy. Before juicing citrus, we always remove the zest, even if the recipe we're making doesn't call for it. Use a **fine-tooth** (**rasp**) **grater** (such as a Microplane) to turn the zest into colorful flavorful granules or a **zester / channel knife** (we like the one from OXO) to shred the zest into tiny curlicues or long thin strips. We add citrus zest to salads, spreads, grilled fish, sautéed veggies, and especially desserts—cakes, cookies, pudding, ice cream, you name it. The strips can be dried on a wire rack at room temperature for about a week and then stored in a closed container for months, ready to add citrus flavor to your cooking any time.

To cut fresh citrus for squeezing, think of the fruit as if it were a globe. When you cut it in half through its equator, you can see a cross section of all the segments inside the fruit, which allows the juice to flow more freely than if you cut the fruit in the other direction (through its axis). Put the citrus halves, cut-side down, in a **citrus squeezer** (we like the one from Bellemain). The squeezer will collapse the fruit, remove most of the juice, and hold back any seeds and pulp.

On the average, 1 lime yields 1 to 2 tablespoons of juice; 1 lemon yields 3 to 4 tablespoons of juice; 1 orange yields 4 to 6 tablespoons of juice, and 1 grapefruit yields about ¾ cup of juice.

DAIRY AND NONDAIRY MILK

Milk is the food that mammals produce to feed their babies. That means that the only "natural" milk is mother's milk. In order to keep drinking milk after weaning, people have come to enjoy milk from other mammals, mostly cows and goats, and also by manufacturing milk from plants. Physically, mammal milk is a liquid emulsion of protein, fat, and sugar suspended in water, and plant milk is a mixture of the same elements extracted from beans, grains, nuts, and/ or seeds into water. All milks are basically interchangeable in any recipe, making allowances for slight differences in fat content and sweetness. If you're using plant milk, use unsweetened and unflavored products unless the recipe specifies otherwise. We used 2% cow's milk in our recipe testing.

OILS

Cuisines are frequently differentiated by the kind of fat they use—butter in most of France, olive oil around the Mediterranean, peanut and sesame oils in China and Southeast Asia, or ghee in the Asian subcontinent. We use olive oil most of the time, grapeseed when we want an oil without much flavor or one that has a high smoke point for frying, and unsalted butter for sweets and most baking.

Olive oil. The flavor of good olive oil is essential to the cooking of the Mediterranean, and it is the oil of choice for most of our recipes. There are lots of classifications for olive oil, mostly about country of origin and how the oil is pressed, although the species of olives is also now included on the label. About 90 percent of the world's olives are pressed for their oil, and most of that oil comes from Spanish Picual olives, which means that even though an oil says it is Italian, it was likely bottled in Italy but not produced in Italy. There are not enough olive trees in all of Italy to account for the amount of olive oil that is labeled "Italian."

To make oil, the olives are ground, pits and all (sometimes with olive leaves, too), and then churned for about half an hour to help release more oil and flavor. To preserve aromatic compounds, the best olive oils are extracted with mechanical pressure as opposed to solvents. Traditionally, a screw press was used, but most olive oil is now extracted by means of a centrifuge. Cold-pressed olive oils are typically extracted at temperatures below 80°F for maximum flavor and minimum free fatty acids, components that can make an oil unstable and prone to rancidity.

Extra-virgin olive oil comes from the most flavorful high-quality olives and contains less than 0.8 percent free fatty acids. The best extra-virgin olive oils are cold pressed without the use of solvents. Virgin olive oil comes from slightly lower-quality olives and contains less than 2 percent acids. Fino olive oil is a mixture of virgin and extra-virgin oils, generally with 2 to 3 percent acids. Pure and pomace olive oils are extracted with solvents, are refined, and have more than 3 percent acids. Light or extra-light olive oil contains a mix of highly refined olive oils to lighten the color (and flavor); it does not contain fewer calories than other olive oils. We use only extra-virgin and virgin olive oils in our recipes.

Grapeseed oil. Grapeseed oil is high in polyunsaturated fats (the kind that are good for lowering blood cholesterol) and has a neutral flavor, which makes it a good oil for adding to sauces, baked goods, and dressing when you want to add richness without introducing new flavors. Grapeseed oil has a relatively high smoke point (the temperature at which oils start to breakdown), 445°F, which makes it a good choice for frying.

Sesame oil. There are two types of sesame oil: toasted sesame oil, also called dark or Asian sesame oil, and light sesame oil, also called plain or white sesame oil. Toasted sesame oil is made from dark roasted sesame seeds and is very flavorful. Its flavor can become bitter when heated too high, so it is almost always used as a finishing oil, or for making uncooked dressings. Light sesame oil is mildly flavored and can be used as you would any neutral oil.

Vegetable oil. Made from a blend of different seeds and fruit, vegetable oil tends to be mild flavored—and inexpensive. It is usually the most cost-effective oil to use for frying or sautéing. The downside of generic vegetable oil is that it is impossible to know exactly what seeds and fruits were processed in its manufacturing. Typically, vegetable oil is predominantly soy, but it could also be a combination of safflower, corn, or sunflower. Canola oil, derived from a variety of seeds from the brassica plant family, which includes mustard, turnip, cabbage, Brussels sprouts, and rutabaga, can be used whenever a recipe calls for vegetable oil.

GARLIC AND ONIONS

Garlic and onions are part of the same botanical genus: *Allium*, which is Latin for "garlic" and includes leeks, chives, shallots, and scallions as well as garlic and onions. All alliums are pungent, and chopping them brings out the pungency. The finer they are chopped, the more flavor they deliver.

Tahini and garlic are historical culinary partners, which is why garlic plays an important part in our recipes. When we call for garlic, we almost always chop it fine or mince it, to release all the flavor it has to give. Although garlic can be minced by food processors, grinders, and garlic presses, all the mechanical options do a more haphazard job and are more tedious to clean than a sharp knife and a cutting board. We recommend mincing garlic with salt, which is what we call for in the recipes.

How to Mince Garlic: It feels a little silly to describe the process, which is simple and takes only a few minutes, but here goes. Place whole cloves on a cutting board. Place the flat side of a broad knife or a heavy skillet on top and whack with the side of your fist. This will crack the papery skin and flatten the garlic a little. Slip the paper peels off and compost or throw into stock. Thinly slice the flattened cloves lengthwise, then slice down the lengths into thin pieces. Scrape the garlic pieces into a pile so that all of the lengths are roughly parallel, then slice across the lengths into pieces of roughly the same size. Scrape into a pile. Sprinkle a large pinch of coarse sea salt over the pile. Chop through the garlic in any direction. The salt will help break down the garlic, and its grit will make the garlic easier to chop. As the pieces spread out, scrape them back into a pile and keep chopping until the garlic pieces are small enough to begin to clump up.

GREEK YOGURT

We like to use Greek yogurt in recipes because it is thicker and creamier than regular yogurt, without added ingredients or chemicals. Like all fermented dairy, yogurt has two parts: curds and whey. Curds are the solid part, and whey is the liquid. Regular yogurt becomes Greek yogurt by draining off much of the whey, resulting in a concentrated form of yogurt that has more protein per spoonful and a thicker consistency. And because so much of the whey has been drained away, Greek yogurt resists separating when it is heated.

MISO

Like any fermented condiment (Worcestershire sauce, soy sauce, pickles), miso punches up the flavor of whatever it touches. Miso is made from mashed soybeans and grain (usually rice and/or barley), mixed with salt and a fermenting fungus, then left for anywhere from a few weeks to a year to ferment into a tangy umami-rich paste. We use it—specifically white miso paste—whenever we need a flavor boost but don't want to push a dish in an herbal or spicy direction. You can find white miso paste in any Asian food market in the refrigerated cases. In conventional supermarkets, it is usually displayed with other international ingredients or alongside plant-based meat products.

NUTRITIONAL YEAST

This deactivated yeast will not make your stomach rise. It is a nutritious powder (or flake) loaded with B vitamins and a strong, protein-rich flavor that is often compared to the flavor of aged cheese—perfect for a vegan queso or Vegan Mac 'n' Cheez (see page 156). It is sold in bulk and prepackaged in most markets and will keep for months in a tightly closed container stored away from heat.

DATE SYRUP (SILAN)

Made by steaming and pressing dates, date syrup (also called "date honey" or "date molasses" and "silan" in Hebrew) is dark brown and complex in flavor, and has been a common sweetener in North Africa and the Middle East for millennia. As a sugar replacement, date syrup is lower in sugar than honey or maple syrup, and higher in magnesium and potassium. Soom sells silan date syrup made from nothing but steamed and pressed dates from the Jordan valley.

RAW SUGAR

When the juice of sugarcane or sugar beets is turned into sugar, it goes through several phases: milling, boiling, and crystallization, which produces a supersaturated dark brown syrup that is seeded with sugar crystals. Once cooled, the sucrose in the syrup forms coarse golden-hued crystals, coated

DEMERARA   PALM SUGAR   TURBINADO

with thick brown syrup (molasses). The molasses-coated crystals can be centrifuged into various types of raw sugar—demerara, turbinado, and muscovado. Palm sugar (aka coconut palm sugar) is raw sugar extracted from the fruit of coconut palms. It is less sweet than other raw sugars.

VINEGAR

Vinegars are made by adding acetic acid–producing bacteria to a fermented alcoholic beverage, like wine, which turns the wine sour, ending up in what the French called *vinaigre*, or "sour wine." We use several types of vinegar in our recipes to add their own distinctive flavor as well as brighten up rich flavors that benefit from an acidic spark. The vinegars we use most often—apple cider vinegar, red wine vinegar, balsamic vinegar, rice wine vinegar, and sherry vinegar—all provide some sweetness as well as acidity.

HERBS AND SPICES

Herbs and spices are the aromatic parts of plants that we use to flavor food. Herbs are the soft parts—leaves and flowers. Spices are the hard parts—seeds, bark, stems, and roots. Spices are always dried and often ground, but herbs can be fresh or dried. Dried herbs are more concentrated, but fresh herbs make up for their lack of strength with fresh vegetal flavor and a more pleasant texture. Because dried herbs and spices have lost their moisture, they need to be cooked in liquid (a sauce or just the juices from sautéing vegetables or roasting meats) in order to rehydrate and release their flavors. Fresh herbs can be added to a recipe near the end. Like fresh vegetables, all they need is a few moments of cooking to release their flavor. Two of our favorite online sources for herbs and spices are Burlap and Barrel (burlapandbarrel.com) and the Reluctant Trading Experiment (reluctantrading.com).

Dried versus Fresh Herbs: We frequently call for fresh herbs, but in a pinch dry can be substituted. As a rule of thumb, dried herbs are three times as pungent as the same herb fresh. That means 1 teaspoon dried herbs = 1 tablespoon fresh herbs.

CARDAMOM

A little camphorous, gingery, and mentholated, cardamom is delicious with a wide range of dishes, both savory (curries and pilafs) and sweet (pastries, puddings, and baked fruit), but be warned—it is very strong, so a little goes a long way. We love it in Cardamom Halvah with Pistachios (see page 194).

CHILES

There are hundreds of types of chiles, and though they all have spicy heat in common, that is not the main reason they appear in these recipes. Besides their heat, chiles are packed with flavor—ancho chiles (dried poblanos) are earthy and mild, chipotle chiles (smoked jalapeños) are smoky and hot, and crushed red pepper (dried cayenne chiles) adds sparks of fire to otherwise homogeneous savory flavored food. Maras (aka Marash) chiles from Turkey and Aleppo chiles from Syria have rich, earthy flavor and a distinctive grainy mouthfeel, popping with bright bursts of crunch—we call for these more than once in our recipes!

Different chiles hit the palate in different places—jalapeños at the tip of the tongue and on the lips, cayenne in the back of the throat, and black pepper all over. When something feels too spicy, it's usually because the movement of the heat across the palate isn't balanced. Too much crushed red pepper (cayenne)? Add some black pepper to bring the heat forward. Too much chipotle? A dash of cayenne will get the heat bouncing back and forth with every bite.

CORIANDER/CILANTRO

Here's one of the few aromatic plants that is both herb (cilantro leaves) and spice (coriander seeds). We use both as often as possible. Cilantro has a unique grassy, insect-like aroma that some people find off-putting but others find addictive. It is assertive, but its flavor is fleeting, especially when cooked. For that reason, cilantro is almost always added near the end of cooking or sprinkled on just before serving. Its ephemeral nature also explains why dried cilantro has practically no flavor at all, so you should use only fresh. Coriander seed smells like lemon oil mixed with sage. It needs heat to release its flavor, so it is usually added early on in a recipe.

CUMIN

Indigenous to the Middle East but used in pretty much every cuisine, cumin is pungent, warm, slightly sweet, and aromatically earthy, with a little pepper-minty aftertaste. The flavor is enhanced by toasting, and the seeds are often heated before grinding. Cumin is a traditional (some would say essential) flavor in tahini sauce and hummus.

MINT

Although there are lots of types of mint, the one that it is most common in the kitchen is spearmint. The flavor is pungent and, well, minty, and is not improved by cooking. For that reason, we almost always scatter chopped fresh mint into a dish just before serving, or sometimes near the end of cooking.

PARSLEY

There are two types of parsley: curly and flat-leaf (aka Italian). Curly parsley is used just as a garnish because it looks nice, thanks to its coarse, frilly structure. Flat-leaf parsley is used for cooking because it is more aromatic and flavorful. Therefore, when we call for parsley in these recipes, we always mean the flat-leaf kind.

ROSEMARY

Rosemary is native to the Mediterranean basin, where it thrives in the sandy soil and misty salt air. When crushed between your fingers, rosemary leaves give off an intense aroma that is piney, cooling, and minty, with hints of eucalyptus that's refreshingly head-clearing. The taste beneath the aroma can be peppery, woody, and warming. Unlike other herbs whose flavors increase when dried, fresh and dried rosemary are equally flavorful.

SUMAC

Sumac (not to be confused with poison sumac, which is never eaten) is the dried berry of the elm-leaved or lemon sumac shrub. It has a sweet and sour flavor, with a strong aroma of lemon oil, and a deep red color. We mix it with dried thyme, dried marjoram, and toasted sesame seeds to make the Middle Eastern spice blend known as za'atar (see page xx) and add it to sauces and main dishes for a spark of tartness.

TURMERIC

Turmeric is a rhizome (part of the root system) of a plant in the ginger family. Like ginger, turmeric is sold in hands (so called because its multi-forked knobs look like fingers). The rhizome is bright orange, and when dried and ground the resulting spice is a deep warm yellow, with an aroma that is both earthy and spicy. Its distinctive hue traditionally dictated that turmeric was a coloring spice, but now that same color is an indication of the presence of beneficial aldehydes that are sought after nutritionally for their powerful antioxidant effect on our cells.

SALT

For the best taste and highest nutrition, our recipes call for sea salt that is simply evaporated ocean water (labeled "pure" or "unrefined"). Sea salts can be ground, either fine or coarse, or they can be left as whole crystals that go by names describing their crystal shape. The most common whole crystal salt is flake salt, which is almost always reserved for finishing. A word of warning: When measuring salt for a recipe, pay attention to its fineness. The finer your salt, the saltier the results. Beautiful handcrafted salts are available online from the Meadow (themeadow.com) and at gourmet stores, like Suraya, a Lebanese specialty market and restaurant in Philly that sells Wajd fleur de sel, a sea salt made in small batches by a family in Koura, North Lebanon.

SESAME SEEDS

Sesame seeds come in two colors, white and black. Toasted white sesame seeds are beige to brown. As you know, tahini is ground toasted sesame seeds, so sesame is obviously a dominant flavor throughout this book. In addition to tahini, we often add sesame seeds to our recipes and use them for garnish. Sesame seeds are high in oil, which means they are prone to turning rancid, so you should only buy an amount you will use up in a few days. For longer keeping, store in the freezer. Toasted sesame seeds are less perishable.

HOW TO USE THIS BOOK

We've organized our recipes into six chapters that capture the everyday opportunities for incorporating tahini into your family's food chain: Savory and Sweet Sauces; Hummus and Other Dips; Breakfast; Sandwiches, Salads, and Sides; Mains; and Sweets. Each chapter includes recipes that range from the tried and true (Lemon Tahini Sauce, Tahini Ranch Dressing, Dark Chocolate Tahini Brownies) to the seemingly elaborate (Roasted Butternut Squash with Orange Tahini, Walnuts, and Za'atar; Roasted Tahini Cauliflower with Pistachios; and Chocolate Halvah French Toast Sandwiches).

We've concentrated on including as many ways that we could think of to stretch the culinary borders of tahini beyond the Middle East. For example, you'll find surprising ways to use tahini in recipes like Vegan Mac 'n' Cheez and No-Mayo Coleslaw. Revolutionizing traditional American staples like these is at the core of our mission. We use tahini to replace eggs, cheese, or cream

to make recipes vegan and/or dairy free. We use it in place of butter to increase the level of polyunsaturated fatty acids in baked goods and sauces, and we add it to all kinds of vegetables to transform side dishes into protein-plentiful mains.

By organizing sauces, dressings, and dips into their own chapter, we hope to encourage home cooks to have a stock of these on hand to instantly turn plainly grilled or roasted vegetables, meats, fish, and poultry into impressive dinners any night of the week.

Regardless of the exotic sound of some of our recipe titles, we are all about quick and easy. We realize that you're busy and the last thing you want to do is linger in the kitchen, but that doesn't mean you don't want a collection of dishes you can feel assured will please sophisticated friends as well as picky kids. Professional culinary terms have been kept to a minimum (and explained when used), and every recipe is streamlined to save time and work.

DIETARY LABEL KEY

When a recipe aligns with a specific diet, the dietary advantage is listed just beneath the title as follows:

V = Vegan   The recipe contains no animal products.

VEG = Vegetarian   The recipe contains no meat or fish, but does contain dairy or eggs.

DF = Dairy Free   The recipe contains no animal milk products.

GF = Gluten Free   The recipe contains no ingredients that regularly include gluten. However, if gluten is a concern, please be sure to check that all packaged products are certified gluten-free, as some things, such as oats, are made in facilities that also process wheat.

FF = Family Friendly   The recipe appeals broadly to a wide array of tastes, specifically children and mature picky eaters.

P = Paleo   The recipe emphasizes animal proteins, vegetables, fruits, seeds, and nuts (foods that would have been hunted and gathered before the advent of agriculture) and avoids foods that are cultivated, like dairy, legumes, and grains.

Tahini has been a staple ingredient in kitchens for millennia. Its benefits and versatility are not new, even though they may be new to you. Tahini's natural nutrition, richness, and delicious flavor make it a super-ingredient to effortlessly expand the way you cook and eat. Take this book as an invitation to bring tahini to your table.

CHAPTER 2

SAVORY AND SWEET SAUCES

LEMON TAHINI SAUCE

V   DF   GF   FF   P

MAKES ABOUT 2 CUPS

This is the mother sauce of Israeli cuisine and an inspiration for thousands of condiments in Israel. If you have only one tahini sauce on hand, this is it.

3 garlic cloves, minced with coarse
  sea salt (see page 18)
¼ cup freshly squeezed lemon juice
1 cup premium tahini paste
1 teaspoon ground cumin
¾ cup ice-cold water

Combine the garlic and lemon juice in a medium bowl. Let it sit for 1 to 2 minutes.

Whisk the tahini and cumin into the garlic mixture until just combined. Don't worry if it gets thick and grainy. Whisk in the water, ¼ cup at a time, until the sauce is smooth and creamy. It should be the consistency of a creamy salad dressing, like ranch.

Store in a closed container in the refrigerator for up to 3 days.

ORANGE-ROSEMARY TAHINI SAUCE

V   DF   GF   FF   P

MAKES ABOUT 2 CUPS

This tastes like Israel. Our parents have an apartment in Jerusalem off Dereh Hevron (the "Road to Hebron"), a street lined with rosemary bushes. Drought-resistant herbs like rosemary grow all over Israel, and their perfume fills the air. Replacing some of the lemon juice that is traditional to tahini sauce with orange makes the sauce mild and naturally sweet.

1 tablespoon extra-virgin olive oil
2 tablespoons finely chopped fresh
  rosemary leaves
2 garlic cloves, minced with coarse
  sea salt (see page 18)
Grated zest and juice of 1 orange
  (about ⅓ cup)
2 tablespoons freshly squeezed
  lemon juice
1 cup premium tahini paste
1 teaspoon ground cumin
¾ cup ice-cold water

Heat the olive oil in a small skillet over medium heat just until warm, less than a minute. Stir in the rosemary, remove from the heat, and give it 10 minutes or so to cool down and get flavorful.

Meanwhile, combine the garlic, orange juice, and lemon juice in a medium bowl. Let it sit for 1 to 2 minutes. Whisk the orange zest, tahini, and cumin into the garlic mixture until just combined. Don't worry if it gets thick and grainy. Whisk in the water, ¼ cup at a time, until the sauce is smooth and creamy. It should be the consistency of a creamy salad dressing, like ranch.

Stir the cooled rosemary oil into the tahini.

Store in a closed container in the refrigerator for up to 3 days.

TURMERIC TAHINI SAUCE

V   DF   GF   P

MAKES ABOUT 2 CUPS

Turmeric has eye-popping color, earthy flavor (sunbaked, a little citrus, a hint of chile), impressive nutritional content (its antioxidants are off the charts), and seemingly limitless versatility. This sauce is a beautiful dip for crudités, makes a great marinade for Mom's Chicken (page 160).

3 garlic cloves, minced with coarse sea salt (see page 18)
¼ cup freshly squeezed lemon juice
1 cup premium tahini paste
1 tablespoon ground turmeric
1 teaspoon ground cumin
1 teaspoon ground coriander
¾ cup ice-cold water

Combine the garlic and lemon juice in a medium bowl. Let it sit for 1 to 2 minutes.

Whisk the tahini, turmeric, cumin, and coriander into the garlic mixture until just combined. Don't worry if it gets thick and grainy. Whisk in the water, ¼ cup at a time, until the sauce is smooth and creamy. It should be the consistency of a creamy salad dressing, like ranch.

Store in a closed container in the refrigerator for up to 3 days.

Tip: This sauce works great as a topping for green or grain salads, grain or noodle bowls, and roasted vegetables.

HERB TAHINI SAUCE

V DF **GF** P

MAKES ABOUT 2 CUPS

Earthy cumin and fresh green herbs? Yes, please. Mix in some chopped jarred artichoke hearts for a sophisticated dip, or use as is to dress any salad.

1 tablespoon extra-virgin olive oil
⅓–½ cup finely chopped fresh basil, parsley, or dill weed in any combination
2 garlic cloves, minced with coarse sea salt (see page 18)
2 tablespoons freshly squeezed lime juice
2 tablespoons freshly squeezed lemon juice
1 cup premium tahini paste
1 teaspoon ground cumin
¾ cup ice-cold water

Heat the olive oil in a small skillet over medium heat just until warm, less than a minute. Stir in the herbs, remove from the heat, and give it 10 minutes or so to cool down and get flavorful.

Meanwhile, combine the garlic, lime juice, and lemon juice in a medium bowl. Let it sit for 1 to 2 minutes.

Whisk the tahini and cumin into the garlic mixture until just combined.

Don't worry if it gets thick and grainy. Whisk in the water, ¼ cup at a time, until the sauce is smooth and creamy. It should be the consistency of a creamy salad dressing, like ranch.

Stir the cooled herb oil into the tahini.

Store in a closed container in the refrigerator for up to 3 days.

ROASTED GARLIC TAHINI SAUCE

V DF **GF** **FF** P

MAKES ABOUT 2 CUPS

Roasting garlic makes your kitchen smell amazing. This creamy, caramel-sweet, garlic-scented spread is also versatile—it's equally sweet and savory.

1 medium head garlic
1 teaspoon extra-virgin olive oil
1 teaspoon coarse sea salt
¼ cup freshly squeezed lemon juice
1 cup premium tahini paste
1 teaspoon ground cumin
¾ cup ice-cold water
2 teaspoons chopped garlic, lightly browned in olive oil, for garnish (optional)

Turn the oven to 375°F.

Cut the pointed top off the head of the garlic, put the head on a square of aluminum foil, and drizzle with the olive oil. Wrap the foil around the garlic and roast the garlic until soft, about 45 minutes. Remove from the oven, unwrap, and let cool.

Squeeze the garlic flesh out of its papery skin into a medium bowl, add the salt and lemon juice, and mash it all together. Let it sit for 1 to 2 minutes.

Whisk in the tahini and cumin until just combined. Don't worry if it gets thick and grainy. Whisk in the ice-cold water, ¼ cup at a time, until the sauce is smooth and creamy. It should be the consistency of a creamy salad dressing, like ranch. Top with the browned garlic (if using).

Store in a closed container in the refrigerator for up to 3 days.

TAHINI MAYO

V   DF   GF   FF   P

MAKES 1¼ CUPS

I love mayo. Probably because it's tangy and creamy, but also because it has so many purposes. I like mixing it with ketchup for burgers or mustard for eggs (think deviled). One of the great things about tahini is that it serves the same purpose as mayo (tangy and creamy), with a helluva lot more nutrition.

- ½ **cup premium tahini paste**
- ¼ **cup freshly squeezed lemon juice**
- ¼ **cup ice-cold water**
- ¼ **cup extra-virgin olive oil**
- ½ **teaspoon fine sea salt**
- ¼ **teaspoon freshly ground black pepper**

Whisk the tahini, lemon juice, water, olive oil, salt, and pepper in a medium bowl until well combined.

Store in a closed container in the refrigerator for up to 1 week.

Tip: This can be used anywhere you'd use traditional mayo.

TAHINI PESTO

VEG   GF

MAKES ABOUT ¾ CUP

Tahini replaces the pine nuts and a lot of the oil in traditional pesto, lending a mildly bitter tang. Use it as you would any pesto—on pasta, grilled fish, pizza, or to jazz up plate of scrambled eggs.

- 2 garlic cloves, minced with coarse sea salt (see page 18)
- 2 tablespoons freshly squeezed lemon juice
- 3 tablespoons premium tahini paste
- 1 cup packed fresh basil leaves (about 1½ ounces)
- 2 tablespoons ice-cold water
- ⅓ cup extra-virgin olive oil
- 3 tablespoons freshly grated Parmesan cheese

Combine the garlic and lemon juice in a food processor. Let it sit for 1 to 2 minutes.

Add the tahini and pulse a few times until just combined. Don't worry if it gets thick and grainy. Add the basil and water and pulse until everything is uniformly green, about 10 pulses. With the processor turned on, drizzle in the olive oil in a slow stream and process until the pesto is smooth and creamy. Scrape into a bowl or storage container and stir in the Parmesan.

Store in a closed container in the refrigerator for up to 3 days.

TAHINI BARBECUE SAUCE

V   DF   GF   FF

MAKES ABOUT 2 CUPS

I've eaten and made more than my share of grilled chicken. And I can say that nothing tops off a chicken over coals better than this barbecue sauce. The seared tahini makes the skin extra crispy, and its nutty creaminess keeps your barbecue from getting too sweet. This recipe whips up in seconds and makes enough for about six pounds of chicken. You can also use it on baked chicken, grilled fish, roasted leg of lamb, or a baked bean casserole.

- ⅔ cup premium tahini paste
- ⅔ cup ketchup
- ½ cup ice-cold water
- 2 tablespoons silan date syrup
- 2 tablespoons apple cider vinegar
- 1½ teaspoons fine sea salt
- 1½ teaspoons smoked paprika
- 1 teaspoon garlic powder
- ½ teaspoon freshly ground black pepper
- ¼ teaspoon chili powder

Whisk the tahini, ketchup, water, date syrup, vinegar, salt, paprika, garlic powder, pepper, and chili powder in a medium bowl until well combined.

Store in a closed container in the refrigerator for up to 1 week.

Tip: This sauce will thicken as it sits. If it gets too thick, adjust its consistency with a small amount of water or fruit juice.

TAHINI STIR-FRY SAUCE

V   DF   FF

MAKES ABOUT 1¾ CUPS

Although tahini is most common in East Mediterranean cooking, there's really no need to keep it there. Sesame is also common in Chinese dishes, and tahini is perfectly at home in a traditionally flavored stir-fry sauce. Use it when wokking-up veggies, poultry, or any meat.

4 garlic cloves, minced with coarse sea salt (see page 18)
1 (½-inch) piece fresh ginger, finely chopped
¾ cup premium tahini paste
¼ cup soy sauce
¼ cup silan date syrup
3 tablespoons ice-cold water
2–3 tablespoons sriracha
2 tablespoons freshly squeezed lime juice
4 teaspoons rice wine vinegar

Whisk the garlic, ginger, tahini, soy sauce, date syrup, water, sriracha, lime juice, and vinegar in a bowl until smooth.

Store in a closed container in the refrigerator for up to 1 week.

Tip: Use this as an all-purpose stir-fry sauce, adding it at the end of stir-frying. No additional thickening is necessary.

CREAMY TAHINI VINAIGRETTE

V   DF   GF   FF   P

MAKES ABOUT 1¾ CUPS

This light and summery vinaigrette is a welcome change from the olive oil and lemon juice dressing typically served on salad—a little creamier, a little heartier. I like to save a scrap of bread just to soak up the puddle left on my plate. It also works great on grilled and roasted meats.

⅓ cup premium tahini paste
2 tablespoons brown or Dijon mustard
1 garlic clove, minced with coarse sea salt (see page 18)
½ cup ice-cold water
⅓ cup freshly squeezed lemon juice
⅓ cup red wine vinegar
⅓ cup extra-virgin olive oil
1½ teaspoons fine sea salt
½ teaspoon freshly ground black pepper

Whisk the tahini, mustard, garlic, water, lemon juice, vinegar, olive oil, salt, and pepper in a medium bowl until smooth and creamy. It should be the consistency of a creamy salad dressing, like ranch.

Store in a closed container in the refrigerator for up to 1 week.

Spicy Tahini Vinaigrette: For a variation with a kick, add 1 teaspoon sriracha and 1 teaspoon silan date syrup or honey before whisking everything together.

TAHINI BALSAMIC DRESSING

V   DF   GF   FF   P

MAKES ABOUT 1 CUP

Your go-to, have-it-in-the-fridge, always-on-hand-for-anything-and-everything, mixes-up-in-a-minute, way-more-than-just-salad-dressing recipe is here. It's also delicious on grilled meat, poultry, or fish.

⅓ cup premium tahini paste
⅓ cup balsamic vinegar
3 tablespoons ice-cold water
½ teaspoon garlic powder
½ teaspoon fine sea salt

Whisk the tahini, vinegar, water, garlic powder, and salt in a medium bowl until well combined.

Store in a closed container in the refrigerator for up to 1 week.

TAHINI RUSSIAN DRESSING

V   DF   GF   FF
MAKES ABOUT 1¾ CUPS

When we were growing up, my dad made us a sandwich of fried kosher salami, coleslaw, and Russian dressing on rye. This Russian is made with tahini instead of mayo and is a must-have for elevating any deli meat sandwich. It can also be used as a dressing for salads or on grilled and roasted meats.

¾ cup premium tahini paste
1 garlic clove, minced with coarse
   sea salt (see page 18)
½ cup ice-cold water
6 tablespoons ketchup
2 tablespoons apple cider vinegar
2 teaspoons dried dill weed
1½ teaspoons fine sea salt
½ teaspoon freshly ground black
   pepper

Whisk the tahini, garlic, water, ketchup, vinegar, dill weed, salt, and pepper in a medium bowl until smooth and creamy. It should be the consistency of a creamy salad dressing, like ranch.

Store in a closed container in the refrigerator for up to 1 week.

SWEET AND SOUR TAHINI DRESSING

V   DF   GF   FF

MAKES ABOUT 1 CUP

This uber tangy dressing is great on potato salad, fried chicken, grilled chicken, leftover steak, corn on the cob, tuna, or anything that says "warm weather" and "picnic."

⅓ cup premium tahini paste
1 garlic clove, minced with coarse sea salt (see page 18)
⅓ cup ice-cold water
2 tablespoons ketchup
2 tablespoons apple cider vinegar
2 tablespoons silan date syrup
1 tablespoon freshly squeezed lemon juice
1½ teaspoons fine sea salt
½ teaspoon freshly ground black pepper

Whisk the tahini, garlic, water, ketchup, vinegar, date syrup, lemon juice, salt, and pepper in a medium bowl until smooth and creamy. It should be the consistency of a creamy salad dressing, like ranch.

Store in a closed container in the refrigerator for up to 1 week.

TAHINI GREEN GODDESS

V   DF   GF   P

MAKES ABOUT 1½ CUPS

Bring this dressing to your next potluck. I guarantee it will go with everything else—on salad, as a dip, on grilled meats, or on tuna.

½ avocado, pitted, peeled, and chopped
⅓ cup premium tahini paste
⅓ cup fresh basil leaves
3 scallions, chopped (green and white parts)
1 garlic clove, chopped
⅓ cup ice-cold water
3 tablespoons extra-virgin olive oil
2 tablespoons freshly squeezed lemon juice
2 tablespoons red wine vinegar
½ teaspoon fine sea salt
¼ teaspoon freshly ground black pepper

In a blender or food processor, combine the avocado, tahini, basil, scallions, garlic, water, olive oil, lemon juice, vinegar, salt, and pepper. Blend until smooth and creamy. It should be the consistency of a creamy salad dressing, like ranch.

Store in a closed container in the refrigerator for up to 1 week.

TAHINI RANCH DRESSING

V   DF   GF   FF

MAKES ABOUT 1¼ CUPS

What's for dinner? Whenever you're making a meal out of the leftovers in the fridge, this is the dressing that ties it all together. And it's the best dip for Tahini Chicken Schnitzel (see page 179).

⅓ cup premium tahini paste
¼ small onion, chopped
1 garlic clove, chopped
⅓ cup ice-cold water
⅓ cup freshly squeezed lemon juice
¼ cup extra-virgin olive oil
2 tablespoons white miso paste
1 tablespoon silan date syrup
1½ teaspoons fine sea salt
1 teaspoon Dijon mustard
½ teaspoon freshly ground black pepper
6 chives, minced

In a blender or food processor, combine the tahini, onion, garlic, water, lemon juice, olive oil, miso, date syrup, salt, mustard, and pepper. Blend until smooth and creamy. It should be the consistency of a creamy salad dressing, like ranch. Stir in the chives.

Store in a closed container in the refrigerator for up to 1 week.

TAHINI MISO SAUCE

V DF GF FF
MAKES ABOUT 1 CUP

Miso is immensely flavorful—tangy, creamy, and umami-rich. This versatile sauce is equally delicious spooned on roasted veggies, grilled chicken breast, or pan-seared fish. It's also a great dip for whatever you got.

3 garlic cloves, minced with coarse sea salt (see page 18)
1 (½-inch) piece fresh ginger, finely chopped
½ cup premium tahini paste
3 tablespoons white miso paste
2 tablespoons freshly squeezed lemon juice
2 tablespoons ice-cold water
1 tablespoon rice wine vinegar

Whisk the garlic, ginger, tahini, miso, lemon juice, water, and vinegar in a bowl until smooth.

Store in a closed container in the refrigerator for up to 1 week.

TAHINI AVOCADO CREAM

V DF GF FF P
MAKES ABOUT 1 CUP

This sauce might remind you of your favorite guac or the green goddess dressing you've been coveting from a favorite restaurant. One advantage it has over both is that the lemon juice and tahini protect the avocado against discoloring. It will stay beautifully green in the refrigerator for a day or more.

½ garlic clove, minced with coarse sea salt (see page 18)
1 large avocado, pitted, peeled, and chopped
Pinch crushed red pepper
2 tablespoons freshly squeezed lemon juice
⅓ cup ice-cold water
2 tablespoons premium tahini paste
2 tablespoons finely chopped fresh cilantro leaves

Put the garlic and avocado in a bowl and mash together with a fork until mostly smooth. Mash in the crushed red pepper and lemon juice. Stir in the water and tahini until smooth. Stir in the cilantro.

Store in a closed container in the refrigerator for up to 2 days.

TAHINI BUTTER

VEG FF

MAKES ABOUT 1 CUP

Use this compound butter to add instant flavor to roast chicken, steamed veggies, baked potatoes, or a thick slab of toast.

1 garlic clove, minced with coarse sea salt (see page 18)
6 tablespoons (¾ stick) unsalted butter, at room temperature
¼ cup premium tahini paste
2 tablespoons freshly squeezed lime juice
2 tablespoons soy sauce
1 teaspoon toasted sesame oil
Fine sea salt and freshly ground black pepper, to taste

Whisk the garlic, butter, tahini, lime juice, soy sauce, sesame oil, salt, and pepper in a small bowl until combined. At first, it looks like this won't happen. Just keep stirring.

Store in a closed container in the refrigerator for up to 2 weeks.

BUFFALO TAHINI SAUCE

V   DF   GF   P

MAKES ¾ CUP

This is as addictive as the buffalo sauce you know and love, but with less saturated fat and completely dairy free. Don't freak out over the amount of hot sauce; just make sure the one you use is on the mild side. Toss with roasted veggies, baste on grilled chicken, or use as a dip with French Fries. I dip my pizza in it.

¼ cup premium tahini paste
¼ cup mild hot sauce, such as
    Frank's RedHot
¼ cup ice-cold water
½ teaspoon fine sea salt

Whisk the tahini, hot sauce, water, and salt in a small bowl until well combined.

Store in a closed container in the refrigerator for up to 1 week.

TAHINI MOLE SAUCE

V   DF   GF   FF

MAKES ABOUT 1¾ CUPS

Mole, the complex nutty-fruity chile sauce from Mexico that is often finished with chocolate, takes a lot of work. But not when you streamline its prep with chocolate tahini—with one ingredient your mole is halfway done. Use to sauce any roasted, sautéed, or fried meat, bird, or fish. Mole is also great with hearty vegetables like baked winter squash, roasted carrots, or sautéed wild mushrooms.

1 tablespoon mild vegetable oil,
    such as grapeseed
3 garlic cloves, minced with coarse
    sea salt (see page 18)
2 teaspoons ground chipotle chile
1 teaspoon ground cumin
½ teaspoon ground cinnamon
3 dates, pitted and minced
1 cup canned crushed tomatoes in
    purée
¾ cup chocolate tahini
½ cup vegetable, chicken, or beef
    broth
2 tablespoons freshly squeezed
    lime juice
Fine sea salt and freshly ground
    black pepper, to taste

Warm the oil in a medium saucepan over medium heat. Add the garlic, chile powder, cumin, and cinnamon and sauté until fragrant, about 30 seconds. Add the dates, tomatoes, tahini, broth, lime juice, salt, and pepper and stir until combined.

Turn down the heat so that the sauce barely simmers and cook until thickened, about 3 minutes. If the sauce gets too thick, adjust the consistency with a few tablespoons of water.

Store in a closed container in the refrigerator for up to 1 week.

SWEET DATE TAHINI SAUCE

V   DF   **GF**   FF   P

MAKES ABOUT 1¼ CUPS

In this recipe, tahini is sweetened naturally with dates and apple juice into an all-purpose sweet sauce, perfect spooned over ice cream, drizzled onto cake or cookies, or basted on chicken wings. Personally, I like to lick it off a finger.

½ **cup premium tahini paste**
¼ **cup apple juice**
2 **tablespoons silan date syrup**
½ **teaspoon fine sea salt**
½ **teaspoon ground cinnamon,**
   preferably Vietnamese
¼ **cup ice-cold water**
3 **pitted Medjool dates, finely**
   chopped

Whisk the tahini, apple juice, date syrup, salt, and cinnamon in a medium bowl until just combined. Don't worry if it gets thick and grainy. Whisk in the water, 1 tablespoon at a time, until the sauce is smooth and creamy. It should be the consistency of a creamy salad dressing, like ranch. Stir in the dates.

Store in a closed container in the refrigerator for up to 3 days.

JAMIE VESPA'S KEBAB SAUCE

V   DF   FF   MAKES ABOUT ¾ CUP

Jamie writes the popular food blog, Dishing Out Health. She is a registered dietitian and has developed some of our favorite recipes for soomfoods.com. This sauce is good on almost anything, but it really shines as a marinade and basting sauce for kebabs. It's also an amazing dressing for kale salad or cold noodle salad (throw in minced candied ginger, sliced scallions, and lots of sesame seeds).

⅓ cup premium tahini paste

3 tablespoons ice-cold water

4 teaspoons sherry vinegar

4 teaspoons silan date syrup

2 teaspoons Asian chili garlic sauce

1 teaspoon soy sauce

½ teaspoon curry powder

½ teaspoon sea salt

Whisk the tahini, water, vinegar, date syrup, chili garlic sauce, soy sauce, curry powder, and salt in a medium bowl until smooth.

Store in a closed container in the refrigerator for up to 1 week.

DARK CHOCOLATE TAHINI SAUCE

VEG   DF   GF   FF
MAKES 1½ CUPS

This mix-it-up-in-a-minute chocolate sauce makes anything from ice cream to strawberries super special. One of my favorite ways to indulge is to peel a clementine or tangerine, set the sections out on a rack for a few hours to get the outsides crispy and their juices concentrated and then sit back and dunk each one in chocolate. Fantastic!

½ cup chocolate tahini
⅓ cup cold heavy cream or nondairy creamer
2 tablespoons silan date syrup
2 tablespoons honey
1 tablespoon Dutch-process cocoa powder
½ teaspoon fine sea salt
3 tablespoons ice-cold regular or decaf coffee
1 ounce dark chocolate, finely chopped

Whisk the tahini, cream, date syrup, honey, cocoa, and salt in a medium bowl until just combined. Don't worry if it gets thick and grainy. Whisk in the coffee, 1 tablespoon at a time, until the sauce is smooth and creamy. Stir in the chocolate. It should be thicker than chocolate syrup but runnier than fudge sauce.

Store in a closed container in the refrigerator for up to 3 days.

TAHINI MAPLE SYRUP

V   DF   GF   FF   P
MAKES ABOUT ½ CUP

Mix it up and drizzle it on pancakes, cut fruit, popcorn, or pretzels, or smear it on hot buttered toast. OMG!

⅓ cup pure maple syrup
¼ cup premium tahini paste
1 teaspoon vanilla extract

Whisk the maple syrup, tahini, and vanilla in a small bowl until well combined.

Store in a closed container in the refrigerator for up to 1 month.

SESAME SALTED CARAMEL SAUCE

VEG GF FF

MAKES 1½ CUPS

I didn't think there was any way to improve on salted caramel. Once again tahini changed my mind.

¼ **cup premium tahini paste**
¼ **cup cold heavy cream**
¼ **cup ice-cold water**
1 **cup granulated sugar**
4 **tablespoons (½ stick) unsalted butter, cut into 12 pieces**
1 **teaspoon coarse sea salt**
1 **teaspoon vanilla extract**
¼ **teaspoon almond extract**

Whisk the tahini and cream in a medium bowl until just combined. Don't worry if it gets thick and grainy. Whisk in the water, 1 tablespoon at a time, until the sauce is smooth and the consistency of softly beaten cream. Set aside.

In a deep, heavy skillet, melt the sugar over medium-high heat to a golden caramel, stirring with a long-handled wooden spoon the whole time. At first the sugar won't do much, but then you'll notice that it gets sticky in spots. Keep stirring and it will soon become pretty lumpy. Keep going and soon the sugar will start to brown and become liquid, with lumps floating in it. You may have to push on the lumps to break them up, but be careful. If the hot syrup splashes on your skin, it will give you a nasty burn.

When the caramel is deep brown and all the lumps have melted, about 4 minutes, turn the heat down to medium-low and stir in the butter until incorporated. Stir in the tahini mixture. The caramel will bubble up; just keep stirring until the bubbling calms down and everything smooths out. Remove from heat and stir in the salt, vanilla, and almond extract.

Store in a closed container in the refrigerator for up to 3 days.

Tip: To make the stored sauce pourable, you will need to warm it up, either on the stove or in the microwave.

CANDIED GINGER TAHINI SAUCE

V   DF   GF

MAKES ABOUT 1 CUP

I love the combination of heat, sweet, and perfume that is ginger. When it's candied, you can add "chewy" to the description, which makes it even better. I like this fragrant sauce warmed up and drizzled over super ripe peaches in the summer or apples and pears when the world turns chilly.

¼ cup premium tahini paste

3 tablespoons freshly squeezed orange juice

3 tablespoons silan date syrup

1 tablespoon grated fresh ginger

1 tablespoon brandy, whiskey, or additional orange juice

2 tablespoons ice-cold water

¼ teaspoon fine sea salt

1 ounce candied ginger, finely chopped (about 2 tablespoons)

Whisk the tahini, orange juice, date syrup, ginger, and brandy in a medium bowl until just combined. Don't worry if it gets thick and grainy. Whisk in the water, 1 tablespoon at a time, until the sauce is smooth and creamy. Stir in the salt and candied ginger.

Store in a closed container in the refrigerator for up to 3 days.

CHAPTER 3

HUMMUS AND OTHER DIPS

ZAHAV HUMMUS

V   DF   GF   FF   SERVES 6 TO 8

I love that Mike Solomonov's hummus completely maxes out on tahini. In the cookbook for Zahav (his award-winning restaurant), he characterizes tahini-heavy hummus as authentically Middle Eastern, and great hummus needs premium tahini for creaminess and flavor. I think it's not an overstatement to say that Zahav changed the way hummus is thought of in the States. I know it changed our life at Soom. This is more or less the Zahav recipe. We add a little more tahini sauce and a little less baking soda.

½ cup dried chickpeas
½ teaspoon baking
    soda
1 cup Lemon Tahini
    Sauce (page 34)
1 teaspoon coarse sea
    salt
¼ teaspoon ground
    cumin

Put the chickpeas in a pint container and fill it with water. Stir in ¼ teaspoon of the baking soda and soak overnight or for at least 8 hours, until they double in size. Drain and rinse.

Put the chickpeas in a medium saucepan and add the remaining ¼ teaspoon of baking soda. Add enough water to cover the chickpeas by about 4 inches. Bring to a boil over medium heat and cook until the chickpeas are completely soft, about 45 minutes, removing any white foam that puffs up on the surface before it boils over. When the chickpeas are done, they will have separated from their skins, and when you taste one, it will be completely smooth—no grit at all. Drain and cool.

In a food processor, combine the chickpeas, tahini sauce, salt, and cumin and purée. Process for twice as long as you think it needs, until the hummus is super smooth.

Store in a closed container in the refrigerator for up to 1 week.

ORANGE-ROSEMARY HUMMUS

V   DF   GF   FF   SERVES 6 TO 8

Many think that hummus is principally chickpeas, but we know that hummus is all about the tahini. Let's be real: Hummus is really just a way to make tahini thick enough to dip. It was a revelation when we mixed our Orange-Rosemary Tahini Sauce into hummus. Unlike traditional tahini, with its strong hits of lemon and garlic, orange-rosemary tahini is super refined and subtle, which transforms this hummus into a truly sophisticated dip.

½ **cup dried chickpeas**
½ **teaspoon baking soda**
1 **cup Orange-Rosemary Tahini Sauce (page 34)**
2 **tablespoons finely chopped fresh rosemary leaves**

Put the chickpeas in a pint container and fill it with water. Stir in ¼ teaspoon of the baking soda and soak overnight or for at least 8 hours, until they double in size. Drain and rinse.

Put the chickpeas in a medium saucepan and add the remaining ¼ teaspoon of baking soda. Add enough water to cover the chickpeas by about 4 inches. Bring to a boil over medium heat and cook until the chickpeas are completely soft, about 45 minutes, removing any white foam that puffs up on the surface before it boils over. When the chickpeas are done, they will have separated from their skins, and when you taste one, it will be completely smooth—no grit at all. Drain and cool.

In a food processor, combine the chickpeas, tahini sauce, and rosemary and purée. Process for twice as long as you think it needs, until the hummus is super smooth.

Store in a closed container in the refrigerator for up to 1 week.

Tip: Instead of soaking dried chickpeas, you can make this hummus with a 15-ounce can of chickpeas. Rinse and drain the chickpeas and toss them with ¼ teaspoon of baking soda in a medium saucepan. Cover them with water and boil until the skins separate and the chickpeas easily break apart when pressed, 10 to 15 minutes.

HUMMUS

with Toasted Chickpeas and Za'atar

V   DF   GF   FF   SERVES 6 TO 8

There are dozens of toasted chickpea and hummus recipes, and all of them claim that the chickpeas get "crispy." Bull! I've tried them all, and though the chickpeas do get roasty-toasty, they're as creamy and yielding as chickpeas always are. Delicious, but definitely *not* crispy.

1½ cups rinsed and drained canned chickpeas or cooked chickpeas

1 tablespoon toasted sesame oil

½ teaspoon coarse sea salt

1 teaspoon Za'atar (recipe follows) or store-bought za'atar

1½ cups Zahav Hummus (page 64), Orange-Rosemary Hummus (page 65), or store-bought hummus

Extra-virgin olive oil, for drizzling

2 tablespoons chopped fresh cilantro

Warm bread, for serving

Turn the oven to 350°F.

Place the chickpeas in a single layer in a folded dry kitchen towel and rub vigorously to get rid of as much of their moisture as possible. Pick out and discard any loose pieces of skin and spread the dried chickpeas on a sheet pan. Drizzle with the sesame oil and season with the salt. Bake until toasted, about 40 minutes.

While still warm, season with the za'atar and let cool. Can be held in a tightly closed container at room temperature away from light for up to 24 hours.

To serve, spread the hummus on a plate in a 1-inch thick layer that is indented in the center. Scatter the toasted chickpeas over the top, concentrating them in the indentation. Drizzle with olive oil. Top with the cilantro and serve with warm bread.

ZA'ATAR

MAKES ¼ CUP

4 teaspoons toasted sesame seeds

1 tablespoon dried sumac

1 tablespoon dried thyme

2 teaspoons dried marjoram

Mix the sesame seeds, sumac, thyme, and marjoram. Store in a tightly closed container away from light for up to 1 month.

CANNELLINI TAHINI

V   DF   **GF**   SERVES 6 TO 8

White beans, the creamiest and mildest of legumes, come in different sizes. Southerners like round pea beans for baked beans, whereas New Englanders prefer to use oval great northern beans. Cannellini beans look like large, pale white kidney beans, and butter beans are cream-colored lima beans. You can use any of them for this super flavorful dip, but cannellini rhymes with tahini, so—decision made!

1 (15-ounce) can cannellini beans, rinsed and drained
1 garlic clove, coarsely chopped
1 teaspoon ground coriander
½ teaspoon ground cardamom
1½ cups Lemon Tahini Sauce (page 34)
¼ cup freshly squeezed lemon juice
2 tablespoons extra-virgin olive oil, plus more for topping
½ teaspoon fine sea salt
1 tablespoon sesame seeds, white or black, or a combination
Pinch crushed red pepper
Warm bread, cut veggies, or wedges of hardboiled egg, for serving

In a food processor, combine the beans, garlic, coriander, and cardamom and pulse to a rough purée, about 4 pulses, scraping down the sides of the bowl once with a silicone spatula. Add the tahini sauce, lemon juice, olive oil, and salt and process until very smooth. Taste and add more salt, if needed.

Transfer to a serving bowl and top with a drizzle of olive oil, sesame seeds, and the crushed red pepper. Serve with bread, veggies, or eggs.

Store in a closed container in the refrigerator for up to 1 week.

SMOKIN' BABA

V DF **GF** P SERVES 4

A fire-roasted eggplant is one of the first things that my brother-in-law, Omri, made for us. He just incinerated it whole over a fire, halved it, and drizzled it with tahini, olive oil, lemon, and salt. Then we dug in. It will always be the definitive food of Israel to me—a luscious smoky pillow on which vibrant fresh flavors love to nestle.

1 large eggplant
½–1 teaspoon fine sea salt
¼ cup Lemon Tahini Sauce (page 34) or Orange-Rosemary Tahini Sauce (page 34)
2 tablespoons finely chopped fresh flat-leaf parsley
1 tablespoon extra-virgin olive oil
1 tablespoon freshly squeezed lemon juice

Set up a grill for high direct heat or turn on the broiler to high.

Poke the eggplant all over with a fork. If grilling, put the eggplant on the grill grate, close the lid, and grill until the eggplant is charred all over, wrinkled, and soft, about 20 minutes, turning halfway through. If using a broiler, put the eggplant on a broiler pan and position the broiler rack so that the eggplant is as close to the heating element as possible without touching it, and broil until charred and soft, about 20 minutes, turning halfway through.

Cool the eggplant until you can touch it comfortably. You can wrap it and refrigerate it for a few hours or overnight to make it easier to handle.

Chop the eggplant so that the skin is in small pieces and the flesh is mushy with just a few strings visible. Stir in the salt, tahini sauce, parsley, olive oil, and lemon juice. Serve with warm flatbread or pita chips.

Store in a closed container in the refrigerator for up to 1 week.

EDAMOLE

V   DF   **GF**   SERVES 6 TO 8

Looks like guacamole, dips like guacamole, but has the protein and hearty texture of hummus. Fluffy, spicy, beany, and not too fatty, this dip is nutritious and filling enough to be a vegan main when accompanied by warm bread and a salad.

2 garlic cloves, peeled and halved

1½ cups frozen shelled edamame, thawed (about 8 ounces)

⅓ cup premium tahini paste

¼ cup water, plus more as needed

¼ cup freshly squeezed lime juice

2 tablespoons extra-virgin olive oil

½ teaspoon hot sauce

1 teaspoon fine sea salt

¼ teaspoon freshly ground black pepper

¼ cup chopped red onion

¼ cup chopped tomato

¼–½ serrano chile, stemmed, seeded, and minced

Tortilla chips and cut veggies, for dipping

In a food processor, combine the garlic, edamame, tahini, water, lime juice, olive oil, hot sauce, salt, and black pepper and purée until smooth and creamy. Add a little more water if it's too thick.

Scrape into a serving bowl and stir in the onion, tomato, and chile. Serve with chips and veggies for dipping.

Store in a closed container in the refrigerator for up to 5 days.

TAHINI GUAC

V   DF   **GF**   **FF**   P   SERVES 6

At Soom, we're obsessed with this guacamole. All of the pleasure of real guac but better.

2 garlic cloves, minced with coarse sea salt (see page 18)

2 ripe avocados, pitted, peeled, and chopped

1 fresh chile, stemmed, seeded, and minced

¼ cup minced red onion

¼ cup freshly squeezed lime juice

3 tablespoons premium tahini paste

2 tablespoons chopped fresh cilantro

1 teaspoon ground cumin

1 tablespoon extra-virgin olive oil

Tortilla chips and cut veggies, for dipping

Mash the chopped garlic, avocados, chile, onion, lime juice, tahini, cilantro, and cumin in a medium bowl with a fork as much as you want, from chunky to smooth. Smooth the top and spread the olive oil over all to keep the guac from discoloring before you serve it.

Serve with chips and veggies for dipping.

Store in a closed container in the refrigerator with a thin film of oil coating the surface for up to 2 days.

VEGAN "QUESO"

V   DF   **GF**   FF   SERVES 6

This isn't exactly like queso made from cheese (there's no melty stretchiness), but the flavor? Kiss your fingertips. The umami in the nutritional yeast paired with the creamy tahini makes this taste like true queso, and it is so easy to throw together, there's no reason to make cheesy queso ever again.

¾ cup salsa
½ cup premium tahini paste
¼ cup ice-cold water
¼ cup nutritional yeast (see page 20)
2 teaspoons ground cumin
½ teaspoon fine sea salt
Tortilla chips, for dipping

In a food processor, combine the salsa, tahini, water, nutritional yeast, cumin, and salt and process until slightly chunky. Pour the mixture into a small saucepan and cook over medium heat, stirring frequently, until just heated through, about 3 minutes.

Serve warm with chips for dipping.

Store in a closed container in the refrigerator for up to 3 days.

PUMPKIN HUMMUS

V   DF   **GF**   SERVES 4

I grew up thinking pumpkins were for carving and pie, nothing else. But when I got to Israel, pumpkin was all over the place, and most of the time it was eaten like other squashes: baked into stews and casseroles, roasted, or fried. When it was puréed, it was more often incorporated into mains than pies. Pumpkin hummus is moister and fresher tasting than typical hummus bi tahini. This one is made with white beans instead of chickpeas for better color and purer vegetable flavor.

1 (15-ounce) can cannellini beans, rinsed and drained

2 dates, pitted and chopped

1 garlic clove, minced with coarse sea salt (see page 18)

½ cup canned pumpkin purée (see tip)

¼ cup premium tahini paste

¼ cup extra-virgin olive oil, plus more for drizzling

½ teaspoon ground cumin

Pinch crushed red pepper

Fine sea salt and freshly ground black pepper, to taste

¼ cup white and black sesame seeds

In a food processor, combine the beans, dates, and garlic and process until mushy. Add the pumpkin purée, tahini, olive oil, cumin, crushed red pepper, salt, and black pepper and process until smooth. Taste and add more salt if needed, pulsing briefly to mix.

To serve, spread the hummus on a serving plate, drizzle with more olive oil, and sprinkle with the sesame seeds.

Store in a closed container in the refrigerator for up to 1 week.

Tip: I know that farmed food is healthy and corporate food is suspect, but canned pumpkin purée is the exception that proves the rule. Pumpkin purée made from scratch is always watery and grainy no matter how long you simmer and strain. Of all the canned options, we've found that Libby's brand gives the best results. This is partially because the canning process helps break down tough fibers and concentrates the flavors of pumpkin more completely than simmering would, but it's also because Libby's is made from a special variety of meaty pumpkin that is unavailable to you and me. I'm not sure why the other brands, regardless of price, organic or not, can't compare.

CAULIFLOWER TAHINI SPREAD

V   DF   GF   P   SERVES 6 TO 8

Anyone who's tried cauliflower rice knows that cauliflower is a chameleon. One of cauliflower's most amazing powers comes from pectin, a starch that is in a lot of fruit and vegetables and makes jellies and jams thick. Cauliflower has a ton of the stuff, which is why you can make a rich creamy spread from it with hardly any fat. Use as a dip for veggies or chips, or as a vegan sandwich spread.

1 medium head cauliflower, leaves and core removed, coarsely chopped
2 garlic cloves, minced with coarse sea salt (see page 18)
¼ cup premium tahini paste
¼ cup white miso paste
2 tablespoons rice wine vinegar
2 teaspoons soy sauce or liquid aminos
1 teaspoon ground turmeric
Pinch crushed red pepper

Bring a pot of salted water to a boil over medium-high heat. Add the cauliflower and simmer until fork-tender, about 8 minutes. Drain and cool for 10 minutes.

Transfer the cooled cauliflower to a food processor. Add the garlic, tahini, miso, vinegar, soy sauce, turmeric, and crushed red pepper and purée until smooth.

Store in a closed container in the refrigerator for up to 1 week.

ROASTED CARROT TAHINI
with Smoked Paprika

V   DF   GF   P   SERVES 6

The gorgeous orange color of this tahini hints at its rich North African flavors. Use as a dip, as a bed for grilled chicken or broiled fish, or as a filling for a pita sandwich.

1 pound carrots, peeled and cut into bite-size pieces

4 garlic cloves, peeled

3 tablespoons extra-virgin olive oil, divided

1 teaspoon ground cumin

½ teaspoon fine sea salt

¼ teaspoon freshly ground black pepper

3 tablespoons premium tahini paste

¼ cup freshly squeezed orange juice

1 tablespoon freshly squeezed lemon juice

1 teaspoon hot sauce

2 tablespoons smoked paprika, divided

Fine sea salt and freshly ground black pepper, to taste

Leaves from 2 mint sprigs, finely chopped

Turn the oven to 400°F.

Toss the carrots and garlic with 1 tablespoon of the olive oil, the cumin, salt, and pepper on a sheet pan. When the oven is up to temp, roast until the carrots are fork-tender, about 30 minutes. Cool for about 5 minutes.

Transfer the roasted carrots to a food processor. Add the tahini, orange juice, lemon juice, 1 tablespoon of the remaining olive oil, the hot sauce, and all but 1 teaspoon of the smoked paprika. Purée until smooth. If it's too thick, add a little water. Taste and season with salt and pepper as needed.

To serve, spread in a wide, shallow bowl, drizzle with the remaining 1 tablespoon of olive oil, and sprinkle with the remaining 1 teaspoon of paprika and the mint leaves.

Store in a closed container in the refrigerator for up to 5 days.

ROASTED BEET HUMMUS

with Pistachio Oil

V   DF   **GF**   SERVES 6 TO 8

The most memorable time I had beets with tahini was our first family meal at Zahav, gorging on Mike's beet tahina salad. I could eat buckets and have done so. That salad inspired this hummus, vibrantly hued and sweet from the beets, and tangy with tahini.

For the beet hummus

1 large beet, scrubbed and trimmed

1 teaspoon extra-virgin olive oil

1 (15-ounce) can chickpeas, rinsed and drained, or 1¼ cups cooked chickpeas

¼ teaspoon baking soda

1 tablespoon chopped fresh rosemary leaves

½ teaspoon fine sea salt

⅛ teaspoon freshly ground black pepper

For the pistachio oil

2 tablespoons extra-virgin olive oil

¼ cup shelled pistachio nuts

1 teaspoon minced fresh rosemary leaves

For serving

Warm flatbread, tortilla chips, and/or cut veggies

Turn the oven to 375°F.

To make the beet hummus: Place the beet on a square of aluminum foil, drizzle with the olive oil, and wrap to seal. Roast the beet until tender, about 1½ hours. Set aside until cool enough to handle but still warm.

Meanwhile, put the chickpeas in a small saucepan. Cover them with about 2 inches of water and stir in the baking soda. Bring to a boil over medium-low heat and cook until the chickpeas are mushy when pressed, about 15 minutes. When you taste one, there should be no sense of grit on your tongue. Drain them and let cool.

When the beet is cool enough to handle, peel off the skin with your fingers or a paring knife. Coarsely chop the beet and transfer it to a food processor. Pulse into a mush. Add the cooked chickpeas, rosemary, salt, and pepper and purée. Process for twice as long as you think it needs, until the hummus is super smooth.

To make the pistachio oil: Just before serving, heat the olive oil in a small skillet over medium heat until just warm, about 1 minute. Stir in the pistachios and rosemary and stir for about 1 minute, until the nuts start to brown a little but not too much. Remove from the heat and give it 10 minutes or so to cool down and get flavorful.

To serve: Spread the hummus on a plate in a thick layer that is slightly indented in the center. Spoon the warm nuts and oil in drizzles over the top. Serve with warm flatbread, chips, or veggies.

Store in a closed container in the refrigerator for up to 5 days.

WARM SPINACH AND FETA TAHINI

VEG | GF | SERVES 6

This tahini is creamy, fluffy, and surprisingly rich without being filling. It makes a great omelet filler.

- 2 garlic cloves, minced with coarse sea salt (see page 18)
- 3 tablespoons premium tahini paste
- 3 tablespoons ice cold water
- 2 tablespoons freshly squeezed lemon juice
- 2 tablespoons extra-virgin olive oil
- 8 ounces baby spinach
- ½ cup crumbled feta cheese, plus more for topping
- 2 teaspoons toasted white or black sesame seeds
- Warm flatbread, tortilla chips, and/or cut veggies, for serving

In a food processor, combine the garlic, tahini, water, and lemon juice and process until smooth.

Heat the olive oil in a large skillet over medium-high heat. Add the spinach and toss until wilted, 1 to 2 minutes. Add to the food processor and pulse a few times, until the spinach is finely chopped. Add the feta and pulse just enough to combine.

Garnish with a little more crumbled feta and the sesame seeds. Serve warm or at room temperature, with warm flatbread, chips, and/or veggies.

Store in a closed container in the refrigerator for up to 4 days.

HUMMUS AND BRIE FONDUTA

VEG GF FF SERVES 6

The oozing melted brie makes this dip unbelievably rich; the hummus keeps it relatively healthy. You will not be able to control yourself. And believe it or not, kids love it!

8 ounces brie
1 cup hummus of your choice
Tortilla chips, flatbread, or crackers, for serving

Remove the rind from the brie and cut the cheese into pieces (it doesn't matter what size). Put the cheese and hummus in a microwave-safe bowl. Microwave at full power for 1 minute, until the cheese melts. Stir with a fork until well combined.

Serve warm with tortilla chips, flatbread, or crackers.

Store in a closed container in the refrigerator for up to 3 days. Rewarm before serving.

CHAPTER 4

〜〜〜〜〜〜〜〜〜〜〜〜

BREAKFAST

TAHINI BENEDICT

VEG **DF** **SERVES 2**

Eggs Benedict is my indulgent restaurant breakfast. I *never* used to make it at home, and not because I can't poach an egg or toast an English muffin. The problem was the hollandaise. It's just too dang tricky—liable to curdle or separate or congeal if you breathe at the wrong time. This blender tahini sauce is a fool-proof substitute for hollandaise.

For the sauce
2 large egg yolks
1 tablespoon freshly squeezed lemon juice
¼ cup premium tahini paste
½ garlic clove, chopped
¼–½ teaspoon sea salt
2–3 tablespoons boiling water

For the eggs
1 tomato, cut into 4 rounds
3 teaspoons extra-virgin olive oil, divided
Fine sea salt and freshly ground black pepper, to taste
½ teaspoon ground cumin
1 tablespoon white vinegar
4 large eggs

To make the sauce: Fill a blender with very hot tap water to warm up the container. Wait 5 minutes, then drain. Add the egg yolks, lemon juice, tahini, garlic, salt and 2 tablespoons boiling water. Blend on medium speed until just combined, about 30 seconds. If the sauce is too thick, add the remaining 1 tablespoon of boiling water and blend to combine. Set aside.

To make the eggs: Turn on the broiler to high and position the broiler rack as close to the heating element as it will go.

Coat the tomato rounds with 2 teaspoons of the oil and set on a broiler pan. Season with salt and pepper and sprinkle on the cumin. Broil until the surface is speckled but the tomato is still firm, about 3 minutes.

Meanwhile, fill a 10- to 12-inch skillet with water and bring to a boil over medium heat. Add the vinegar.

Crack each egg into a separate cup or ramekin. Gently slip each egg from its cup into the water. Turn the heat to medium-low so that the water in the pan barely simmers.

For assembly
**2 English muffins, split
and toasted**
**½ cup pickled red
onion, carrot, or
radish (page 127)**

Poach the eggs until the whites are set and the yolks remain creamy, about 2 minutes.

To assemble: Put an English muffin on each plate. Top each half with a broiled tomato. Use a slotted spatula to remove each egg from the water, wait a few seconds to let any extra water drain back into the pan, then place it on the tomato. Top each with sauce and a little pile of pickled red onion. Serve immediately.

Tip: About one in every twenty thousand eggs is contaminated with harmful salmonella microorganisms. If you buy your eggs from a reliable source and are careful to keep them refrigerated, you should not have a problem. Bacteria are destroyed through pasteurization. By adding boiling water to the egg yolk that is going into a sauce, you semi-pasteurize it, thereby greatly reducing even the slim chance that a foodborne illness could be a problem. If you have a compromised immune system, you should avoid eating eggs that are less than hard cooked.

MAPLE TAHINI GRANOLA

V   DF   **GF**   FF   SERVES 4

Before I learned this recipe, my granola was always store-bought. Not anymore. You'll need about 45 minutes, but all but a few of those are spent baking. Don't try speeding it up. The secret to scrumptious granola is controlling the heat so that the grain doesn't get too dark. This recipe is cane sugar–free, getting all of its sweetness from pure maple syrup.

2 cups old-fashioned oatmeal
½ cup sliced almonds
½ cup walnut pieces
½ cup white sesame seeds
½ teaspoon ground cinnamon
Large pinch fine sea salt
6 tablespoons pure maple syrup
¼ cup premium tahini paste
2 tablespoons coconut or nut oil
½ cup chopped dried apples, apricots, or raisins

Turn the oven to 250°F.

Mix the oatmeal, almonds, walnuts, sesame seeds, cinnamon, and salt in a large bowl. Mix the maple syrup, tahini, and oil in a small bowl, then pour over the oat mixture. Toss until everything is well coated.

Scrape onto a rimmed sheet pan with a silicone spatula. Pack into an even layer. Bake until the granola is golden, about 40 minutes, flipping and flattening with the spatula halfway through.

Set aside to cool. Break the granola into chunks and toss with the dried fruit.

Store in a tightly closed container at room temperature for up to 3 weeks.

OVERNIGHT OATMEAL

V   DF   **GF**   **FF**   SERVES 1

Mix up this streamlined version of muesli (Swiss granola) before going to bed for an instant breakfast packed in its own transportable container.

⅓ cup old-fashioned oats

2 tablespoons sesame seeds

1 teaspoon ground cinnamon, preferably Vietnamese

¼ teaspoon ground allspice

3 pitted dates or dried apricots, chopped

6 pecans or walnut halves, chopped

½ cup dairy or nondairy milk of choice

1 tablespoon premium tahini paste

2 teaspoons silan date syrup or honey

Put the oats, sesame seeds, cinnamon, allspice, dates, pecans, milk, tahini, and date syrup in a pint-size mason jar and stir to combine.

Cover and refrigerate overnight, or at least 4 hours. Serve in the morning. Warm it up in the microwave before serving, if you want.

TAHINI PANCAKES

with Date Syrup

VEG   FF   SERVES 4 OR 5

I grew up on pancake mix, but I've since learned that scratch is so simple. I love being able to alter the results by changing white flour to whole wheat or by throwing in a handful of oats. This recipe adds nuttiness and nutrition by replacing the oil with tahini. We even whip up our own date and tahini syrup.

For the syrup
½ cup silan date syrup
¼ cup premium tahini paste
1 teaspoon vanilla extract
¼ teaspoon fine sea salt
4 Medjool dates, pitted and finely chopped
1–2 tablespoons fruit juice of choice or water

For the pancakes
½ cup whole-wheat flour
¼ cup granulated sugar
¼ cup old-fashioned oats
2 teaspoons baking powder
Pinch fine sea salt
1 large egg, beaten
¾ cup 2% milk
¼ cup premium tahini paste
2 tablespoons unsalted butter, plus more for serving
1 tablespoon mild vegetable oil, such as grapeseed

To make the syrup: Mix the date syrup, tahini, vanilla, and salt in a small bowl with a fork or small whisk to combine. Stir in the dates. Adjust the consistency with the fruit juice. Set aside.

To make the pancakes: Turn the oven to 200°F.

Mix the flour, sugar, oats, baking powder, and salt in a large bowl. Mix in the egg, milk, and tahini until just combined.

Melt the butter and oil in a large skillet over medium-high heat. Pour the batter, ¼ cup at a time, into the hot pan, leaving about an inch between each pancake. Cook until the tops become bubby, about 2 minutes. Flip the pancakes and cook on the other side until brown, about 1 more minute. Keep the pancakes warm in the oven while you repeat the process with the remaining batter.

Serve warm with the syrup and more butter.

CINNAMON "BABKA" FRENCH TOAST

VEG   FF   SERVES 4

Babka, the thickly swirled cinnamony-nutty-raisiny-chocolaty coffee cake that crowned the counter of every Jewish deli of my childhood, makes the *best* French toast. Topping soft, rich challah French toast with a pile of buttery chocolate tahini crumbs resurrects the babka of my childhood, without having to go out and buy a babka.

8 (½-inch-thick) slices challah or brioche bread
4 large eggs
2 cups 2% milk
½ teaspoon vanilla extract
½ cup granulated sugar
4 teaspoons ground cinnamon, divided
¼ cup all-purpose flour
¼ cup almond meal or other nut meal
¼ cup light or dark brown sugar
1 tablespoon cocoa powder
Pinch fine sea salt
4 tablespoons (½ stick) unsalted butter
¼ cup premium tahini paste
¼ cup raisins, chopped
2 tablespoons mild vegetable oil, such as grapeseed

Let the bread slices sit out overnight to get a little stale or bake them in a 200°F oven for 10 minutes to dry the surface. Cool to room temperature.

Turn the oven to 300°F.

Beat the eggs in a glass baking dish large enough to hold the challah slices in a single layer. Mix in the milk, vanilla, sugar, and 1 teaspoon of the cinnamon. Add the stale bread and soak, turning once or twice so that all of the slices are coated evenly, until all of the liquid is absorbed.

While the challah is soaking, mix the flour, almond meal, brown sugar, cocoa powder, and salt in a medium bowl.

Melt the butter in a large skillet over medium heat. Pour half of the melted butter into the flour mixture. Add the remaining 3 teaspoons of cinnamon and the tahini to the flour mixture, stirring with a fork until it becomes a mass of sticky crumbs, just a few minutes. Stir in the raisins.

Add the oil to the butter in the skillet and heat over medium-high heat until the butter bubbles. Brown the soaked bread on both sides, a few at a time. Transfer the toast to a sheet pan or shingle in a baking dish.

Scatter the chocolate tahini crumbs over the top and bake until the bread is bouncy in the center and the topping has slumped over the French toast, about 10 minutes. Serve.

CHOCOLATE HALVAH FRENCH TOAST SANDWICHES

VEG · **FF** · SERVES 4

The secret to great French toast is stale bread. Bread that has lost a lot of moisture is thirsty, eager to suck up the rich flavorful custard you soak it in. In this recipe, the richness is amped up by making chocolate sandwiches from the bread before soaking.

16 (¼-inch-thick) slices challah or brioche bread
½ cup chocolate tahini
3 large eggs
2 cups dairy or nondairy milk of choice
2 teaspoons honey
1 teaspoon vanilla extract
1 teaspoon ground cinnamon
Pinch fine sea salt
2 tablespoons unsalted butter
2 tablespoons mild vegetable oil, such as grapeseed
¼ cup premium tahini paste
¼ cup silan date syrup
3 tablespoons freshly squeezed orange juice

Leave the bread out overnight so that it dries out a little, or toast it lightly.

Turn the oven to 200°F.

Spread half the bread slices with the chocolate tahini and make them into sandwiches with the remaining slices. Press down on the top of each sandwich to help it hold together.

Mix the eggs, milk, honey, vanilla, cinnamon, and salt until combined in a baking dish large enough to hold the sandwiches in a single layer. Lay the sandwiches in the egg mixture, turning them once or twice to coat evenly. Set aside to soak, turning once or twice, until all of the liquid has been absorbed by the bread.

Melt the butter and oil in a large skillet over medium heat. Working in batches, cook the soaked sandwiches until they are golden brown on both sides and their middles feel springy when pressed, about 4 minutes per side. Transfer to a sheet pan and set in the oven to keep warm while browning the rest of the sandwiches.

Mix the tahini, date syrup, and orange juice in a small bowl until smooth. Serve two French toast sandwiches per person, drizzled with some tahini syrup.

TAHINI ENERGY BARS

V   DF   GF   FF   MAKES 16 BARS

Energy bars have gotten really pricey, and most are loaded with sugar. These are easy to make (no baking), and they last for two weeks, ready to pull out of a backpack or a pocket when you need some quick nutrition to get up and go. You can use any oil, but I prefer coconut.

2 cups old-fashioned oats

½ cup silan date syrup or honey

½ cup premium tahini paste

2 tablespoons coconut oil

1 teaspoon vanilla extract

16 Medjool dates, pitted and chopped

1½ cups puffed rice cereal

1 cup toasted (or black) sesame seeds

¼ teaspoon fine sea salt

Turn the oven to 325°F.

Put the oats in an 8- or 9-inch-square baking pan. Bake until the oats are lightly toasted, about 15 minutes. Set them aside to cool.

Meanwhile, mix the date syrup, tahini, and oil in a small saucepan over low heat and warm until combined and bubbling, about 3 minutes. Remove from the heat and stir in the vanilla.

Toss the dates, cereal, sesame seeds, and salt in a large bowl. Add the toasted oats and mix until everything is well distributed.

Line the bottom of the same baking pan with parchment paper or aluminum foil.

Add the tahini mixture to the oat mixture and, using your hands, mix until everything is well combined. Transfer the mixture to the prepared pan and pack it in. Moisten your hands with cold water to pat everything down and even out the surface.

Refrigerate for about 2 hours to set. Cut into 16 bars and wrap each one tightly in plastic.

Store in the refrigerator for up to 2 weeks.

TAHINI DOUGHNUTS

with Tahini Glaze

VEG   FF   MAKES 9 DOUGHNUTS

When it comes to doughnuts, freshness rules but fades fast. Once it's gone, a doughnut might be good, but it can't be stellar. These doughnuts take only about 10 minutes of active work, but the dough has to chill for an hour or so to firm enough to handle easily. If you want them for breakfast, you can mix up the dough the night before and refrigerate them overnight. Then just cut, fry, and dig in.

For the dough

- 2¼ cups cake flour, plus more as needed
- 1½ teaspoons baking powder
- ½ teaspoon fine sea salt
- 1 teaspoon ground nutmeg
- ⅓ cup firmly packed light brown sugar
- 2 tablespoons unsalted butter, at room temperature
- 3 large eggs
- ½ cup premium tahini paste
- Mild vegetable oil, such as grapeseed, for frying

For the glaze

- 1½ cups confectioners' sugar
- ¼ cup chocolate tahini
- ¼ cup 2% milk or water
- ½ teaspoon vanilla extract

To make the dough: Mix the cake flour, baking powder, salt, and nutmeg in a medium bowl to combine.

In a stand mixer fitted with the paddle attachment, beat the brown sugar and butter until blended. Add the eggs and beat on medium speed until combined, about 1 minute. Add the tahini and beat for 30 seconds. It may look split, but it will get smooth when you add the flour mixture.

Beat in the flour mixture until just combined. Scrape the dough onto a large sheet of plastic wrap. Pat the dough into a round and wrap the plastic around it. Refrigerate for 1 hour to firm.

To make the glaze: While the dough chills, whisk the confectioners' sugar, chocolate tahini, milk, and vanilla in a small bowl until smooth.

To make the doughnuts: Remove the dough from the fridge. Dust a work surface with a little flour and pat the dough out into a rough 9-inch square, about ½ inch thick. Cut the dough into 9 squares. Don't worry if they're not perfect. Use a small twist-off bottle cap to cut a hole in the middle of each doughnut. (Save the middles to make doughnut holes.)

recipe continues ▷

Use a small sharp knife to score the tops of the dough-nuts in the shape of a square around the holes. Transfer the doughnuts to a sheet pan and refrigerate for 30 minutes.

Pour about 4 inches of oil in a large, heavy-bottomed pot. It shouldn't come more than halfway up the sides. Heat over medium heat until an instant-read thermometer stirred through the oil reads 350°F.

Add 3 doughnuts, scored-side up and fry until they float, about 45 seconds. Flip and cook for 1 minute, or until browned underneath, then flip again and fry for another 1 minute on the first side. Using tongs or a slotted spoon, transfer the doughnuts to a plate lined with paper towel to drain. Repeat with the remaining doughnuts in two more batches, making sure to return the oil to 350° each time.

Dip the scored side of each doughnut in the glaze. Turn them glazed-side up and let the glaze set for about 10 minutes. Serve right away.

TAHINI BANANA BREAD

VEG   DF   **FF**   SERVES 8

The top of this extravagant yet healthy sweet bread is striped with a sliced banana and polka-dotted by white and black sesame seeds. It looks awesome but tastes even better—nutty from the tahini, with a jolt of toasted sesame oil.

For the banana bread

Cooking spray, for greasing
2 large eggs
1 cup granulated sugar
⅔ cup premium tahini paste
4 very ripe (lots of brown spots) bananas, peeled and mashed, plus 1 ripe (but not too ripe) banana, peeled and sliced
7 tablespoons mild vegetable oil, such as grapeseed
1 tablespoon toasted sesame oil
1 teaspoon vanilla extract
1 teaspoon ground cinnamon
½ teaspoon fine sea salt
2 cups unbleached all-purpose flour
1 teaspoon baking powder
1 teaspoon baking soda
1 teaspoon black sesame seeds
1 teaspoon white sesame seeds

For the glaze (optional)

3 tablespoons confectioners' sugar
2 tablespoons premium tahini paste
1 tablespoon hot water

To make the banana bread: Turn the oven to 350°F. Grease a 9 × 5-inch loaf pan with cooking spray, line the bottom with parchment paper, and spray the parchment with cooking spray. If you don't have parchment paper, you can dust the interior of the pan with flour after spraying it.

In a stand mixer fitted with the paddle attachment (or in a large bowl with a whisk), beat the eggs and granulated sugar vigorously until pale and fluffy, about 3 minutes. Stir in the tahini, mashed bananas, vegetable oil, sesame oil, vanilla, cinnamon, and salt.

Mix the flour, baking powder, and baking soda in a medium bowl. Add the flour mixture to the batter in two additions, mixing until just smooth after each. Don't overdo it. Pour and scrape the batter into the prepared pan, then sprinkle the top with the sesame seeds. Shingle the sliced banana down the center; you may not need the whole banana.

Bake until a skewer inserted in the center comes out with a few moist crumbs clinging to it, about 1 hour 10 minutes.

Cool the bread in the pan for 15 minutes. Remove from the pan, then transfer to a wire rack to cool completely.

To make the glaze: If using, mix the confectioners' sugar, tahini, and water in a small bowl until smooth. Drizzle over the top of the bread.

CHOCOLATE HALVAH LATTE

V   DF   GF   FF   SERVES 2

Hot chocolate just grew up. The addition of tahini gives it a rich, smooth mouthfeel, sort of like drinking a bar of chocolate halvah. I listed the cocoa powder and cinnamon as optional, but trust me, you'll want to use them.

2 cups dairy or nondairy milk of choice

2 tablespoons extra-fine (Turkish grind) dark roast coffee

3 tablespoons chocolate tahini

1 teaspoon cocoa powder (optional)

¼ teaspoon ground cinnamon, preferably Vietnamese (optional)

Combine the milk and coffee in a small saucepan over medium heat. Simmer and stir for 1 minute. Add the tahini and whisk vigorously until the tahini is melted and the mixture is foamy.

Divide between two coffee cups and sprinkle with the cocoa and cinnamon (if using).

TAHINI, BANANA, AND DATE MILKSHAKE

V   DF   GF   FF   P   SERVES 2

The typical milkshake goes down with a hefty dose of guilt. There's too much cream, too much sugar, and too much indulgence. This shake takes out all the bad stuff, replacing the sugar with fruit and the ice cream with a frozen banana and a dollop of tahini. It tastes like you're being bad, but your body will thank you.

2 ripe (but not too ripe) bananas, peeled and sliced

1½ cups dairy or nondairy milk of choice

⅓ cup premium tahini paste

6 Medjool dates, pitted and torn in pieces

¼ teaspoon vanilla extract

Dash almond extract

Pinch ground cinnamon, preferably Vietnamese

1 teaspoon toasted sesame seeds

Lay the banana slices in a single layer on a sheet pan and freeze until solid, about 1 hour.

Transfer the frozen bananas to a blender. Add the milk, tahini, dates, vanilla, almond extract, and cinnamon and blend until smooth. Add an ice cube or two if you want to lighten it.

Pour into glasses, sprinkle the sesame seeds on top, and serve with a spoon to stir and scoop.

TAHINI TURKISH COFFEE LATTE SHAKE

V   DF   GF   FF   P   SERVES 2

Tahini sweetened by date syrup and frozen with milk is amazingly like premium ice cream. Here the mix is flavored with finely ground coffee (coffee and tahini are a magical combo) and a sprinkle of cardamom (cardamom and coffee are a classic Turkish combo) and then blitzed into a slurpable shake. This is our facsimile of what they make at Goldie, a popular Israeli-style falafel restaurant in Philly.

⅓ cup premium tahini paste
¼ cup silan date syrup
2 cups dairy or nondairy milk of choice
Pinch fine sea salt
1 tablespoon ground Turkish coffee or other finely ground coffee
Pinch ground cardamom

In a blender, blitz the tahini, date syrup, milk, and salt until smooth. Pour the mixture into an ice cube tray and freeze until solid, at least 2 hours or up to several weeks.

When ready to serve, transfer the tahini ice cubes to the blender and add the coffee and cardamom. Blend until smooth and thick. Pour into chilled glasses and serve.

CHAPTER 5

SANDWICHES, SALADS, AND SIDES

BAKED FALAFEL SANDWICHES

V DF **FF** SERVES 4

Falafel are almost never made at home (even in the Middle East), so in that way this recipe is not traditional. It also defies convention because the fritters are baked rather than fried. Way healthier, way easier, and way less messy! I encourage you to make fresh pita, as it's best served up chewy and warm—prebaked packaged pita can't compare. The dough is not special, but the way it's formed and baked is. My trick? Premade refrigerated pizza dough and a hot oven.

For the falafel

- 1 cup dried chickpeas
- 4 tablespoons extra-virgin olive oil, divided
- 4 garlic cloves, coarsely chopped
- 1 small carrot, peeled and chopped
- 1 small onion, chopped
- 2 teaspoons fine sea salt
- 2 teaspoons ground cumin
- 1 teaspoon ground turmeric
- 1 teaspoon ground coriander
- ½ teaspoon freshly ground black pepper
- Pinch ground cayenne pepper
- Pinch ground cinnamon
- Large handful fresh flat-leaf parsley
- Large handful fresh cilantro

To make the falafel: Put the chickpeas in a quart container and fill it with water. Soak overnight or for at least 8 hours, until they double in size. Drain and rinse.

Turn the oven to 375°F. Coat a rimmed sheet pan with 3 tablespoons of the olive oil.

In a food processor, combine the drained chickpeas, garlic, carrot, onion, salt, cumin, turmeric, coriander, black pepper, cayenne, cinnamon, parsley, cilantro, and remaining 1 tablespoon of olive oil. Pulse until the chickpea mixture is very finely chopped and sticks together when pinched.

Scoop about 2 tablespoons of the chickpea mixture with your hand or a small ice cream scoop. Form into a 1½-inch-thick patty and put it on the oiled sheet pan. Do the same with the rest of the chickpea mixture. You will have 12 patties.

Bake until browned on both sides, about 25 minutes, turning halfway through.

For assembly

4 Fresh-Baked Pitas (recipe follows) or store-bought pitas

1–1½ cups tahini sauce of choice (pages 34–61)

1–2 cups tossed green salad, Greek Salad (page 133), or Chopped Salad (page 139)

To assemble: Cut one end from each pita. Spread a dollop of the tahini sauce in the pita and add two falafel, a small handful of the salad, another falafel, and another dollop of tahini sauce. You can also cut the pita in half and fill each half with salad, tahini sauce, and 1½ falafel. Do the same with the rest of the pita, falafel, tahini sauce, and salad. Serve.

Tip: The falafel can be baked ahead and rewarmed for 1 minute in the microwave.

FRESH-BAKED PITA

MAKES 4 PITAS

1 pound refrigerated bread or pizza dough

Mild vegetable oil, such as grapeseed, for greasing

Turn your oven to as high as it will go. Put a large cast-iron skillet on a rack in the center of the oven.

Divide the dough into four pieces and roll each piece into a ball. Cover and let rest for 20 minutes as the oven heats up. Lightly grease a work surface with vegetable oil and roll one of the dough balls out to an 8-inch-wide, ⅛- to ¼-inch-thick disk. Oil both sides of the dough round. Do the same with the rest of the dough.

Put one dough round on the hot skillet and close the oven door. Bake until puffed and brown, about 5 minutes. Transfer to a wire rack and repeat with the remaining dough rounds.

QUICK PICKLE AND TAHINI GUAC SANDWICH

VEG   DF   MAKES 1 SANDWICH AND ABOUT 1 CUP OF EACH PICKLE

These directions make one sandwich, but about a cup of three different pickles. That's so you always have them on hand, for munching, making sandwiches, bowls, or salads, or dressing up a hummus platter. Jarred pickles are too salty. Make your own with whatever veggies you've got on hand, and you control the freshness and flavor. Eating is getting so much better!

¼ cup Tahini Guac (page 77) or any hummus or spread (pages 64–90)
2 slices whole-grain bread, toasted
1 small Persian or Kirby cucumber, thinly sliced
2 lettuce leaves, cut to fit the bread
Quick Pickles (recipe follows)

Spread the guac on the toast slices. Top one with cucumber, lettuce, and some of each pickle. Top with the other bread slice, guac-side down. Halve and serve.

QUICK PICKLES

VEG   DF   GF   P   ABOUT 3 CUPS

6 carrots, peeled and julienned
1 red onion, peeled and very thinly sliced
12 red summer radishes, trimmed and thinly sliced
1½ cups apple cider vinegar
1½ cups water
6 tablespoons honey
1 tablespoon fine sea salt
½ teaspoon crushed red pepper

Put each of the cut veggies in their own pint container.

In a small saucepan, combine the vinegar, water, honey, salt, and crushed red pepper and bring to a boil over medium-high heat. Pour a third of the pickling mixture over each of the veggies. Let cool for about 30 minutes before serving.

Store in closed containers in the refrigerator for up to 2 weeks.

TUNA, TAHINI, AND AVOCADO TOAST

DF   FF   SERVES 2

This is all about me! For one, I'm definitely a member of the avocado toast generation, but I've never really grown out of the years when I ate a tuna sandwich every day for lunch. This sandwich spans my lifetime. All I had to do was add tahini.

1 (5-ounce) can tuna in water, drained
1 celery rib, finely chopped
½ cup Lemon Tahini Sauce (page 34), divided
1 avocado, pitted and peeled
½ garlic clove, minced with coarse sea salt (see page 18)
2 teaspoons extra-virgin olive oil, divided
2 thick slices whole-grain bread, toasted
Coarse sea salt and freshly ground black pepper, to taste
2 tablespoons chopped fresh cilantro leaves
Pinch crushed red pepper

In a small bowl, mix the tuna, celery, and ¼ cup of the tahini sauce. In another small bowl, mash the avocado with the back of a fork, mixing in 1 tablespoon of the remaining tahini sauce.

Mix the garlic with 1 teaspoon of the olive oil and rub it all over one side of each piece of toast.

Divide the tuna mixture evenly between the toasts and top with the avocado mixture. Season generously with salt and pepper. Drizzle with the remaining 3 tablespoons of tahini sauce and the remaining 1 teaspoon of olive oil. Top with the cilantro and crushed red pepper and serve.

TAHINI FIG TOAST

VEG **SERVES 1**

PB&J is kid's stuff. Tahini fig toast, spread on pan-toasted artisan bread, drizzled with date syrup, and embittered by orange marmalade is an adults-only edible form of ecstasy.

1 tablespoon unsalted butter, at room temperature

1 thick slice crusty bread

2 tablespoons premium tahini paste

1 tablespoon plus 1 teaspoon silan date syrup, divided

1 tablespoon orange marmalade

1 dried fig, coarsely chopped, or 1 fresh fig, thinly sliced

Large pinch coarse sea salt

Spread the butter on both sides of the bread and toast in a heavy skillet over medium-high heat, about 2 minutes per side.

While the bread is toasting, mix the tahini and 1 tablespoon of the date syrup in a small bowl.

Spread the toast with the tahini mixture. Top with the marmalade and fig. Drizzle with the remaining 1 teaspoon of date syrup and season with salt. Serve.

GREEK SALAD
with Tahini Dressing
VEG **GF** **SERVES 4**

When I was growing up, my family went out to eat Greek a lot. Every Saturday after basketball games, our mom would take us to a Greek restaurant, so whenever I dig in to a Greek salad I think of her.

For the dressing

1 cup Creamy Tahini Vinaigrette (page 42)

1 tablespoon plain Greek yogurt

½ teaspoon dried oregano

For the salad

6 cups baby spinach (12 ounces)

3 cups baby arugula (2 ounces)

¼ cup packed mint leaves, coarsely chopped

2 tablespoons finely chopped fresh dill weed

1 roasted red pepper, seeded, peeled, and finely chopped

¼ medium red onion, finely chopped

12 Kalamata olives, pitted, halved lengthwise, and sliced

To make the dressing: Whisk the tahini vinaigrette, yogurt, and oregano in a large salad bowl until well combined.

To make the salad: Add the spinach, arugula, mint, dill, red pepper, onion, and olives to the bowl with the dressing. Wash your hands and toss the salad gently by hand until all of the dressing at the bottom of the bowl has been dispersed, and everything is nicely coated. Wash your hands again and serve.

COLD SPICY SESAME NOODLES

V DF SERVES 4

Even though tahini screams Middle East, sesame doesn't. Sesame seeds and sesame oil are equally at home in Scandinavia and Southeast Asia. These noodles, dressed with date-sweetened sesame paste, spiced with soy and Thai fish sauce, are decidedly Asian inspired. The salad is great for lunch or dinner, and the noodles paired with the dressing are a complete protein.

1 (8- to 9.5-ounce) package dried soba noodles

¼ cup premium tahini paste

1 garlic clove, finely chopped

¼ cup rice vinegar

2 tablespoons soy sauce

2 tablespoons Thai fish sauce

1 tablespoon silan date syrup

2 tablespoons mild vegetable oil, such as grapeseed

1 tablespoon toasted sesame oil

2 cups baby spinach

1 avocado, pitted, peeled, and diced

1 cup shredded carrot or jicama

2 scallions, finely sliced (green and white parts)

2 tablespoons Gomashio (recipe follows) or store-bought gomashio

Cook the soba noodles as directed on the package. Drain and rinse in a colander until cool.

In a large serving bowl, whisk the tahini, garlic, vinegar, soy sauce, fish sauce, date syrup, vegetable oil, and sesame oil until well combined.

If the noodles have clumped up, run cold water over them and separate with your fingers. Shake off all excess water from the noodles, then add them to the dressing. Add the spinach, avocado, carrot, and scallions and toss to coat well. Sprinkle the gomashio on top and serve.

Tip: You can find gomashio (sometimes spelled *gomasio*) at any Asian grocery store, Whole Foods Market, or online.

Gomashio: Toast 1 cup sesame seeds in a hot cast-iron skillet until aromatic. Scrape into a grinder and cool. Add 1½ tablespoons coarse sea salt to the hot skillet and cook over medium-high heat until it starts to gray. Grind the seeds coarsely and mix with the salt. Store at room temp for up to 2 months.

KALE AND CANNELLINI SALAD

with Garlic Ranch Tahini

VEG **GF** **SERVES 4**

When we demo Soom in stores, we're always looking at what people have in their carts; it's our form of guerilla market research. It's startling how many are buying kale. As sisters, we don't agree on much, but we all concur that kale is, well, challenging. It's sort of tough and rough and aggressively green. But it's amazing suffused with tahini dressing. Massaging in the dressing softens kale's hard edges and relaxes its oh-so-good-for-you righteousness.

1 bunch kale, locanto or curly

½ cup premium tahini paste

¼ cup freshly squeezed lemon juice

1 tablespoon plain Greek yogurt

1 teaspoon brown mustard

½ cup water, as needed

1 teaspoon minced garlic clove

2 tablespoons chopped fresh flat-leaf parsley

1 tablespoon chopped fresh dill weed

¼ teaspoon freshly ground black pepper

2 clementines

½ roasted red pepper

1 (15-ounce) can cannellini beans, rinsed and drained

½ medium red onion

Fine sea salt, to taste

Tear the leafy parts of the kale from the thick central stems. Discard the stems or save to cook with other greens. Tear the leaves into tiny pieces and put them in a salad bowl.

Whisk the tahini, lemon juice, yogurt, and mustard in a small bowl until well combined. A little at a time, whisk in enough of the water to make the dressing creamy and pourable. Stir in the garlic, parsley, dill, and black pepper.

Pour the dressing over the kale and massage it into the kale until the leaves are saturated with dressing, about 2 minutes. Let it rest for at least 20 minutes or as long as 2 hours.

Peel and section the clementines. Discard any seeds and large pieces of charred skin from the roasted red pepper, and chop it. Chop the red onion finely.

About 10 minutes before serving, add the clementines, red pepper, beans, and onion and toss to combine. Season with salt to taste. Serve.

JULIE'S CREAMY TAHINI CAESAR SALAD

SERVES 4

We are always trying to eat more salads at work, so Julie Ozlek, our digital marketing manager, set out to "Soom-up" a Caesar salad recipe. We've shared it with the Soom community and it's a hit. Pretty straightforward and completely delicious.

For the dressing

2 garlic cloves, chopped

½ cup premium tahini paste

½ cup plus 2 tablespoons ice-cold water, plus more if needed

3 tablespoons freshly grated Parmesan cheese

3 tablespoons freshly squeezed lemon juice

1½ teaspoons Dijon mustard

½ teaspoon apple cider vinegar

½ teaspoon fine sea salt

¼ teaspoon freshly ground black pepper

For the salad

Leaves from 2 romaine hearts, or 1 large head romaine lettuce, torn into small pieces

As much sliced cucumber, diced avocado, quartered cherry tomatoes, Parmesan cheese, croutons, grilled chicken or salmon as you want

To make the dressing: In a blender or food processor, combine the garlic, tahini, water, Parmesan, lemon juice, mustard, vinegar, salt, and pepper. Blend until combined. If the consistency is too thick, add more water as needed.

To make the salad: Place the romaine hearts and any or all of the other ingredients you want in a large serving bowl. Add the dressing and toss to coat. Serve right away.

CHOPPED SALAD

with Date Tahini Vinaigrette

V   DF   **GF**   **FF**   **P**   SERVES 6

Chopped salad, also known as Israeli or Arabic salad, is straightforward: tomato, cucumbers, and onion. This one goes rogue by adding some sweetness in the form of apples and dates. Still traditional, but also a little out there.

1 teaspoon sea salt

1 garlic clove, minced

¼ cup freshly squeezed lemon juice

6 pitted Medjool dates, finely chopped

3 Persian or Kirby cucumbers, finely chopped

2 celery ribs, finely chopped

1 medium tomato, finely chopped

1 apple, cored and finely chopped

½ small red onion, finely chopped

1 tablespoon premium tahini paste

2 teaspoons silan date syrup

1 teaspoon extra-virgin olive oil

½ teaspoon freshly ground black pepper

½ cup chopped flat-leaf parsley

Mix the salt, garlic, and lemon juice in a small bowl until combined and let it sit for 10 minutes or so.

Toss the dates, cucumbers, celery, tomato, apple, and onion in a salad bowl to combine.

Whisk the tahini, date syrup, olive oil, and pepper into the garlic mixture until smooth. Add the vinaigrette to the salad mixture and toss. Taste and season with salt and pepper as needed.

Cover and refrigerate for at least 20 minutes or up to 24 hours. Stir in the parsley just before serving.

SALT-BAKED BEET SALAD

with Tahini and Mint

V   DF   GF   P   SERVES 4

Mike Solomonov taught us about baking beets in salt, which makes them way tastier than either boiling or roasting. The beets shrivel a little, because the salt sucks out some of their moisture. The loss of water concentrates their sugars, and the hint of salt makes that extra sweetness extra delicious. There's no need to peel the beets ahead of time. The peel slips off easily when they come out of the oven.

4 cups coarse sea salt, plus more to taste

5 medium beets, roots trimmed

½ cup tahini sauce of choice (pages 34–61)

¼ cup freshly squeezed lemon juice

3 tablespoons extra-virgin olive oil

3 tablespoons chopped fresh mint leaves

Turn the oven to 375°F.

Pour 2 cups of the salt into an 8- or 9-inch-square baking pan. Nestle the beets, pointed-side up, in the salt, then cover them with the remaining 2 cups of salt, letting it mound up around the beets.

Roast until the largest beet can be pierced easily with a fork, about 2 hours. Set the beets aside until they are cool enough to handle but still warm, about 30 minutes.

Remove the beets from the salt and peel them with a small sharp knife. Let them cool completely, then shred on the large-tooth side of a box grater.

Transfer the shredded beets to a bowl. Add the tahini sauce, lemon juice, olive oil, and mint. Season with salt to taste and serve.

Tip: Cooking anything in an oven concentrates its flavor. Adding salt increases the concentration and sends the flavor into the stratosphere. Baking in salt is a cooking technique that likely predates the oven. Humans were evaporating salt from ocean water since before recorded history, and most cuisines have at least one dish that is baked encased in sea salt. The salt seasons the surface of the food, but more importantly it absorbs any moisture that escapes from the food during baking, keeping the surface dry, increasing surface crispness, and eliminating any tendency for the baking food to become soggy.

TAHINI-DRESSED TUNA, CHICKEN, EGG, OR WHATEVER SALAD

DF GF FF P SERVES 2

Tahini is a natural replacement for mayonnaise. So whatever your reason—health, change of pace, or you just don't dig mayo—this recipe is for you. Whipping up a quick tahini sauce ups the nutrition of your everyday tuna, chicken, or egg salad—a small change with a great effect.

1 small garlic clove, minced with coarse sea salt (see page 18)

1 tablespoon freshly squeezed lemon juice

¼ cup Tahini Mayo (page 39)

½ teaspoon brown mustard

½ teaspoon ground cumin

1 (5-ounce) can tuna, drained and flaked apart, or 1 cup chopped cooked chicken, or 4 hard-boiled eggs, chopped

½ cup finely chopped celery

1 scallion, finely chopped (green and white parts)

Mix the garlic and lemon juice in a medium bowl and let it sit for 10 minutes or so.

Stir in the tahini mayo, mustard, and cumin. Add the tuna (or chicken or eggs), celery, and scallion and mix until just combined. Serve.

NO-MAYO COLESLAW

VEG   DF   **GF**   FF   SERVES 4

The best trick to improve your favorite coleslaw is to add the salt to the cabbage instead of to the dressing. Salting crisp watery veggies (like cabbage or cucumbers) before adding them to a salad keeps them from watering down the dressing as the salad sits. Don't worry about making the salad too salty. After salting, you will wring out the excess water, and the salt will flow away with the water.

- 3 cups shredded coleslaw mix or finely shredded cabbage
- ½ teaspoon fine sea salt
- 2 tablespoons freshly squeezed lime juice
- 1 tablespoon premium tahini paste
- 1 tablespoon extra-virgin olive oil
- 1 tablespoon apple cider vinegar
- 1 tablespoon honey
- ½ teaspoon hot sauce (optional)
- ¼ teaspoon freshly ground black pepper
- 1 medium carrot, peeled and shredded
- ¼ medium red onion, finely sliced
- ¼ cup chopped fresh flat-leaf parsley
- 2 tablespoons toasted sesame seeds

Toss the coleslaw mix with the salt in a large bowl. Set aside until the coleslaw looks pretty wet, about 20 minutes. Transfer the coleslaw to a clean tea towel. Wrap the towel up around the coleslaw and squeeze over a sink, extracting as much liquid as you can.

While the coleslaw is salting, whisk the lime juice, tahini, oil, vinegar, honey, hot sauce (if using), and pepper in a serving bowl until combined. Add the wrung coleslaw, carrot, onion, and parsley and toss until everything is well coated.

Refrigerate for about 30 minutes, then scatter the sesame seeds over the top just before serving.

Store in a closed container in the refrigerator for up to 1 day.

SESAME SLAW

VEG   DF   **FF**   SERVES 6

This is an awesome slaw for grilled chicken or Black Bean Tahini Burgers (see page 168). The ingredients are Asian inspired, but the results go with any cuisine. It's pretty, too—a tangle of pale cabbage shreds, with hints of red radish and yellow-green avocado peeking through.

½ **head napa cabbage, finely shredded (about 1 pound)**

2 **teaspoons coarse sea salt**

2 **tablespoons soy sauce**

1 **tablespoon rice vinegar**

1 **tablespoon premium tahini paste**

1 **tablespoon toasted sesame oil**

½ **teaspoon honey**

4 **red radishes, halved lengthwise and thinly sliced**

½ **avocado, pitted, peeled, and chopped**

3 **tablespoons sesame seeds**

Toss the cabbage with the salt in a serving bowl. Set aside until the cabbage looks pretty wet, about 20 minutes. Transfer the cabbage to a clean tea towel. Wrap the towel up around the cabbage and squeeze over a sink, extracting as much liquid as you can.

Rinse out the bowl and add the soy sauce, vinegar, tahini, sesame oil, and honey; mix until combined. Stir in the wrung cabbage, radishes, avocado, and sesame seeds and toss to combine.

Store in a closed container in the refrigerator for up to 1 day.

SWEET TAHINI ROASTED CARROTS

VEG   DF   GF   FF   SERVES 4

Cooking most vegetables kills some of their vitamins. But with hard vegetables like carrots, cooking relaxes the tough fibers, making their nutrition much more available to your digestive system. Roasting concentrates the sweetness of carrots and caramelizes their sugar, giving them a "meatier" taste.

2 tablespoons extra-virgin olive oil, divided

1½ pounds carrots, peeled and cut into equal pieces

½ teaspoon fine sea salt, divided

⅓ cup freshly squeezed orange juice, divided

2 tablespoons premium tahini paste

2 tablespoons honey

1 teaspoon smoked paprika

1 teaspoon ground turmeric

¼ teaspoon freshly ground black pepper

Pinch crushed red pepper

2 tablespoons chopped fresh flat-leaf parsley and/or cilantro

2 tablespoons crumbled feta (optional)

Turn the oven to 375°F. Coat the bottom of a rimmed sheet pan with 1 tablespoon of the olive oil.

Put the carrots on the pan in a single layer and roll them around in the oil to coat. Season with ¼ teaspoon of the salt. Roast until barely browned, about 30 minutes.

While the carrots are roasting, whisk ¼ cup of the orange juice, the tahini, honey, paprika, turmeric, black pepper, crushed red pepper, and remaining ¼ teaspoon of salt in a medium bowl until well combined.

Pour the tahini sauce over the carrots and toss to coat the carrots well. Roast for another 10 minutes.

Drizzle the remaining orange juice and olive oil over the carrots, then sprinkle the parsley and feta (if using) on top. Serve right away.

Tip: There are four families of colorful pigments in vegetables: Chlorophyll is green, carotene is yellow to orange, anthocyanin is red to purple, and flavone is pale yellow to white. They are present in all vegetables. including carrots. Which pigment shows can be manipulated by cultivation. Carrots are orange when carotene dominates, purple when anthocyanins are bred to emerge, and pale white when both are suppressed. You can switch up the color of carrots in any recipe. Besides providing visual interest, vegetable pigments are loaded with phytochemicals that fight cell degradation.

ANA SORTUN'S TAHINI CREAMED GREENS

V   DF   GF   P   SERVES 4

Ana Sortun, owner of Oleana and Sofra Bakery and Café, was named Best Chef in the Northeast by the James Beard Foundation in 2005. She is known for her passion for Turkish cooking, spices, and fresh organic vegetables from Siena Farms, the family farm owned by her husband, Chris Kurth, and named after their daughter. Sortun's use of tahini to replace cream and rendered fat in these greens is inspirational. Serve as a side dish to roast chicken or grilled fish; these greens are also delicious as a tart filling or piled on a thick slice of toasted bread.

For the tahini sauce
- 2 tablespoons premium tahini paste
- 2 tablespoons extra-virgin olive oil
- 1 tablespoon freshly squeezed lemon juice
- 1 small garlic clove, minced with coarse sea salt (see page 18)
- ½ teaspoon ground cumin

For the greens
- 2 pounds leafy greens, like spinach, broccoli rabe, black kale, or Swiss chard
- 2 tablespoons extra-virgin olive oil
- 2 garlic cloves, minced
- 2 tablespoons freshly squeezed lemon juice
- Coarse sea salt, to taste
- Pinch ground Maras or Aleppo chile (see page 24)

To make the tahini sauce: Whisk the tahini, olive oil, lemon, garlic, and cumin in a small bowl until smooth.

To make the greens: Cut out and discard any thick stems from the greens. Heat the oil in the largest skillet you have over medium-high heat, about 30 seconds. Add the greens and garlic, tossing to coat everything with oil. Cover the pan and cook until the greens wilt, 2 to 4 minutes, depending on the toughness of the greens. Uncover the pan and cook until the greens are just tender and most of the liquid has evaporated.

Stir in the tahini sauce and lemon juice. Taste and season with salt as needed. Sprinkle with the chile and serve.

Tip: You always want to measure greens by weight because the volume of one type of green can be radically different from another. For example, a pound of raw spinach looks like a lot more than a pound of chard, but spinach shrinks more in cooking, so the volumes even out.

CHAPTER 6

MAINS

VEGAN MAC 'N' CHEEZ

V   DF   **FF**   SERVES 6

Mac and cheese undermines the best parental intentions—the box kind is just too available, too easy, and too often becomes the go-to last-minute dinner. One of the things we love about tahini is that it gives creaminess to recipes that call for cream or milk. While this recipe isn't as quick as the boxed schlock, it's super easy, insanely delicious, and much more nutritious. Kids scarf it down!

4 tablespoons vegetable oil, divided

2 large Yukon Gold potatoes, peeled and diced

2 large carrots, peeled and diced

½ medium onion, diced

1 small garlic clove, minced

1½ cups water

Coarse sea salt and freshly ground black pepper, to taste

1 (12-ounce) box elbow macaroni

⅓ cup premium tahini paste

3 tablespoons nutritional yeast (see page 20)

1 tablespoon malt or apple cider vinegar

2 teaspoons brown mustard

1 teaspoon ground turmeric

1 teaspoon sweet paprika

Bring a large pot of water to a boil.

Meanwhile, heat 1 tablespoon of the oil in a large skillet over medium-high heat. Add the potatoes, carrots, and onion and sauté until the vegetables lose their raw look, about 4 minutes. Stir in the garlic. Add the water, salt, and black pepper. Stir to moisten everything, reduce the heat to a simmer, then cover and simmer until the vegetables are very tender, about 10 minutes. Uncover the pot. If there is still water in the pan, continue to cook until it has boiled off, but the veggies should still look soft and moist.

The pot of water should be boiling now. Add a small handful of salt. Add the macaroni and stir until the water returns to a boil. Cook the macaroni until tender, about 5 minutes. Drain the macaroni, reserving 1 cup of the pasta water.

While the macaroni is cooking, scrape everything from the skillet into a food processor. (You can also use a blender, but because this mixture is thick, a processor will make the job easier.) Add the remaining 3 tablespoons of oil, the tahini, nutritional yeast, vinegar, mustard, and turmeric. Pulse until smooth.

Combine the cooked macaroni and the blended "cheez" sauce in a serving bowl and mix well. If the mixture is too thick, thin with a little of the reserved pasta water. Sprinkle the top with the paprika and serve.

ROASTED BUTTERNUT SQUASH
with Orange Tahini, Walnuts, and Za'atar

V   DF   **GF**   **FF**   **P**   SERVES 6

Wildly pretty and so easy, these vegetables can be roasted ahead. Simply refresh them in the microwave or a warm oven and finish with the sauce, freshly toasted nuts, freshly chopped herbs, and toast made from a crusty artisanal bread.

1 (2-pound) butternut squash, peeled, seeded, and cut into wedges

5 tablespoons extra-virgin olive oil, divided

2 large leeks, cut into 1-inch pieces (white and pale green parts)

¼ cup premium tahini paste

5 tablespoons freshly squeezed orange juice

2 tablespoons freshly squeezed lemon juice

1–2 tablespoons water

1 garlic clove, minced

½ teaspoon fine sea salt

⅛ teaspoon crushed red pepper

⅓ cup chopped walnuts

2 tablespoons chopped fresh flat-leaf parsley

1 tablespoon Za'atar (page 69) or store-bought za'atar

Flake salt and freshly ground black pepper, to taste

Turn the oven to 475°F.

Toss the squash with 2 tablespoons of the olive oil on a large sheet pan. Roast until the squash starts to brown, about 15 minutes. Toss the leeks with 1 tablespoon of the remaining oil and add to the pan of squash. Roast until the squash is tender enough to pierce easily with a knife, about 15 minutes more.

While the vegetables roast, whisk the tahini and orange and lemon juices in a small bowl. Add enough water to make the mixture the thickness of cream sauce. Season with the garlic, fine sea salt, and crushed red pepper.

Heat 1 tablespoon of the olive oil in a small skillet over medium-high heat. Add the walnuts and stir until they darken slightly and smell toasty. Scrape into a bowl, cool for a bit, and toss with the parsley and za'atar.

When the vegetables are done, transfer them to a platter. Season with flake salt and black pepper. Drizzle with the tahini sauce and remaining 1 tablespoon of olive oil, and scatter the walnut mixture on top. Serve right away.

Tip: If you have some Orange-Rosemary Tahini Sauce (see page 34) hanging out in the fridge, you can use ¾ cup of that instead of making the sauce in this recipe.

MOM'S CHICKEN

with Turmeric Tahini, Chickpeas, and Onions

DF **GF** FF SERVES 4

This easy sheet-pan dinner exudes exotic aromas and makes an exciting colorful presentation. It smells like the butter chicken I get from my favorite Indian restaurant. As it roasts, the sauce sets up on the chicken, giving you a thick, crunchy-on-the-edges, chewy-moist-in-the-middle texture—amazing.

1 (3½- to 4-pound) chicken, cut into parts, or 3 pounds bone-in, skin-on chicken parts

Coarse sea salt and freshly ground black pepper, to taste

2 cups Turmeric Tahini Sauce (page 35), divided

2 (15-ounce) cans chickpeas, rinsed and drained

1 medium red onion, thinly sliced, divided

1 tablespoon ground turmeric

1 teaspoon ground cumin

1 teaspoon ground coriander

2 tablespoons extra-virgin olive oil, divided

1 tablespoon freshly squeezed lemon juice

Coarsely chopped leaves from ½ bunch cilantro

¼–½ teaspoon hot sauce

Rub the chicken pieces with a generous amount of salt and pepper and put in a large zip-top plastic bag with 1 cup of the tahini sauce. Seal the bag, leaving one corner open about ½ inch. Massage the bag to coat all of the chicken pieces with sauce, then squeeze as much air as you can out of the bag and seal the bag completely. Let it sit out for 30 minutes, or overnight in the refrigerator.

Turn the oven to 425°F.

Toss the chickpeas and half of the onion with the turmeric, cumin, and coriander on a large sheet pan. Drizzle with the olive oil, season with salt and pepper to taste, and toss everything to coat. Push everything to the edges of the pan and put the chicken pieces in the center in a single layer. Bake until the onions are crisp, the chicken skin is brown, and an instant-read thermometer registers 160°F when inserted into the thickest part of a thigh, about 50 minutes.

While the chicken is cooking, toss the remaining onion with the lemon juice and season with salt and pepper.

When the chicken is done, transfer it to a serving plate along with the chickpeas and onions. Drizzle with some of the remaining 1 cup of tahini sauce and the hot sauce. Scatter the onion-lemon mixture and cilantro on top. Serve any remaining tahini sauce on the side.

Leftover Chicken Salad with Chickpeas and Dates:
For this leftover variation, combine any remaining
chicken, chickpeas, and onion with a handful of quartered dates, diced cucumber or celery, and sliced scallion or diced red onion in a serving bowl. In a separate
bowl, combine any leftover tahini sauce with some
apple cider vinegar, date syrup, and salt and pepper.
Add the dressing to the salad and toss to combine.

WHOLE BAKED FISH

with Tahini, Sweet Garlic, and Pistachios

DF **GF** **P** SERVES 2

Wanna be fancy? Try this. It's surprisingly easy considering the impressive results. Don't be intimidated at the thought of cooking a whole fish—the flesh stays flavorful and moist when it's cooked on the bone, and slashing the skin makes it easy to portion and serve. Tonight is special.

For the fish
- 1 tablespoon extra-virgin olive oil, plus more for greasing
- 1 (1½-pound) whole pompano, red snapper, or black bass, gutted and cleaned
- Coarse sea salt and freshly ground black pepper, to taste

For the sauce
- ¼ cup premium tahini paste
- 1 garlic clove, pressed or minced
- ¼ cup freshly squeezed lemon juice
- 1 tablespoon Thai or Vietnamese fish sauce
- 2 teaspoons silan date syrup
- Coarse sea salt and freshly ground black pepper, to taste
- 2–3 tablespoons ice-cold water

Turn the oven to 450°F. Put a wire rack on a rimmed sheet pan or use a broiler pan. Grease the rack with a dribble of olive oil.

To make the fish: Scrape the dull side of a knife against the skin of the fish, running from tail to head, to remove excess moisture and lingering fine scales. Cut 3 or 4 diagonal slices into the skin and through the flesh of the fish on each side, down to the bone. Season the fish inside and out with salt and pepper and rub the olive oil over the outside. Transfer the fish to the prepared wire rack. Bake the fish for about 25 minutes, flipping after 15 minutes, until the thickest part of the flesh flakes when gently pressed with a finger.

To make the sauce: While the fish is baking, whisk the tahini, garlic, lemon juice, fish sauce, date syrup, salt, and pepper in a small bowl until combined. Add the water, 1 tablespoon at a time, and whisk until it is the consistency of unbeaten cream. Let it sit.

For the topping

1 tablespoon extra-
   virgin olive oil
3 garlic cloves, thinly
   sliced
1 tablespoon coarsely
   chopped pistachios
   or pine nuts
2 teaspoons silan date
   syrup or honey
1 tablespoon chopped
   fresh flat-leaf parsley
Large pinch coarse
   sea salt

To make the topping: Warm the oil in a small skillet over medium-high heat. Add the garlic and stir until just beginning to color, about 20 seconds. Add the pistachios and sauté until everything is medium brown, about 2 minutes. Remove the skillet from the heat and stir in the date syrup, parsley, and salt.

When the fish is done, transfer it to a serving platter using one large or two regular spatulas. Generously drizzle some sauce over the fish and serve the rest on the side. Scatter the topping over all and serve the fish by lifting sections from the bone with a small spatula at the diagonal cuts. There is no reason to remove the skin. The skin on any of the recommended fish is perfectly edible. When you have served the top side of the fish you can either lift the skeleton from the bottom side using two forks or flip the fish to serve the remaining side.

Tip: Your fish seller will clean the fish for you, so there's no need to work yourself up about gutting and scaling. Granted, serving fish from the bone is more complex than slipping a fillet onto a plate, but you can do that anytime. (If you still don't want to cook a whole fish, you can use any thick, meaty fish fillet, like salmon, tuna, cod, or halibut. If you do, reduce the baking time to 15 minutes.)

BLACK BEAN TAHINI BURGERS

with Tahini Mayo and Sesame Slaw

VEG   DF   FF   SERVES 4

Meatless burgers are everywhere. Even meat-eaters are switching over. These days when you're doing a cookout, you gotta have a vegan option, and these burgers are it. The deep red beet gives them a meaty appearance, and the mashed black beans, rich tahini, and chewy quinoa lend the sensation of biting into a beef burger. The smoky seasoning and cooking on a grill deliver a fire-pit dining experience. I know this looks like a long recipe—it's a lot of ingredients but not a lot of work. Everything just gets thrown together and grilled, and if you want to make the burgers without the slaw, go for it.

1 tablespoon extra-virgin olive oil

1 small red onion, finely chopped

1 cup finely chopped mushrooms

1 teaspoon ground cumin

1 teaspoon smoked paprika

1 teaspoon fine sea salt

½ teaspoon freshly ground black pepper

1 (15-ounce) can black beans, rinsed and drained

¾ cup cooked quinoa or other grain

1 cup finely shredded raw red beet

¼ cup premium tahini

1 tablespoon soy sauce

½ cup finely ground walnuts (you can grind walnuts in a food processor)

Set up a grill for medium direct heat (350°F to 400°F). You can also use a cast-iron skillet on the stove, in which case preheating is unnecessary.

To make the burgers, heat the olive oil in a large skillet over medium-high heat. Add the onion and mushrooms and sauté until most of the water has evaporated, about 8 minutes. Remove from the heat and season with the cumin, paprika, salt, and pepper. Add the black beans and mash with the back of a fork into a chunky purée. There should be no whole beans, but there should still be lots of visible chunks. Stir in the quinoa, beet, tahini, soy sauce, walnuts, and flaxseed. Chill for 10 minutes. Form the mixture into four patties about ¾ inch thick. Coat with the vegetable oil and set aside on a plate or sheet pan.

Put a grill screen on the grill and coat with oil. Heat for at least 5 minutes. Or heat a large cast-iron skillet over medium-high heat and coat the bottom of the pan with oil. Put the burgers on the hot pan; close the grill cover with the vents completely open or cover the skillet. Cook the burgers until browned and heated through, about 5 minutes per side. During the last minute, toast the cut surface of the buns.

⅓ cup ground flaxseed meal

¼ cup mild vegetable oil, such as grapeseed, plus more for cooking

4 burger buns, split

½ cup Tahini Mayo (page 39) or regular mayonnaise

1 teaspoon chipotle hot sauce

1 teaspoon smoked paprika

1 cup Sesame Slaw (page 147) or No-Mayo Coleslaw (page 146)

To assemble the burgers, mix the tahini mayo, hot sauce, and paprika in a small bowl. Spread a thin layer of the mixture on the cut sides of the buns. Top the bottom halves with burgers, a little more mayo, and a generous dollop of the slaw. Place the bun top on top. If you have more slaw than can fit on the burgers, serve the rest on the side.

PILE-IT-ON FLATBREAD

with Pomegranate and Green Tahini Sauce

DF SERVES 6

Bear with me. This recipe has a lot of steps and ingredients, but I promise it's worth it. Yes, there are several components—pulled meat, savory onions, and tangy pomegranate sauce—but you make all of them in one pot as the meat slowly cooks until it's incredibly tender and juicy. Once the meat is done, you just separate the components and pile them on warm pita. It's my favorite way to eat.

1 teaspoon ground cumin

1 teaspoon ground coriander

1 teaspoon curry powder

1 teaspoon crushed dried rosemary

1 teaspoon coarse sea salt

1 teaspoon freshly ground black pepper

½ teaspoon crushed red pepper

2 pounds boneless, skinless chicken thighs, beef brisket, or boneless leg of lamb

2 tablespoons extra-virgin olive oil

3 onions, halved and thinly sliced

3 garlic cloves, sliced

2 cups pomegranate juice

2 tablespoons honey

Mix the cumin, coriander, curry, rosemary, salt, black pepper, and crushed red pepper in a small bowl. Rub half of the spice mixture all over the meat and set the rest aside. Wrap the meat in plastic wrap and refrigerate for 24 hours.

Turn the oven to 200°F.

Heat the olive oil over medium-high heat in a Dutch oven or deep skillet large enough to hold the meat snugly. Add the meat and brown on all sides. Transfer to a plate.

Add the onions to the pan and sauté, stirring often, until browned, about 10 minutes. Add the remaining spice mixture and garlic and sauté until aromatic, a few seconds. Return the meat to the pan, along with any juices that have collected on the platter. Pour in the pomegranate juice and bring it to a boil. Cover the pan and bake until the meat is fork-tender, about 1 hour for chicken, 4 to 5 hours for beef or lamb.

Turn the oven up to 400°F. Ladle the meaty pomegranate juices into another skillet, leaving the onions and meat behind. Return the meat to the oven, uncovered, and bake until the top of the meat is crisped, about 5 minutes for chicken, 15 minutes for beef or lamb.

6 Fresh-Baked Pitas (page 125), or store-bought

1½ cups Herb Tahini Sauce (page 38) or Tahini Green Goddess (page 46)

½ cup pomegranate seeds

¼ cup chopped fresh mint leaves

Meanwhile, skim any fat from the meaty pomegranate juices and discard. Stir in the honey. Boil over medium-high heat until the liquid is reduced to 1½ cups, about 10 minutes.

Transfer the meat to a cutting board, leaving the onions in the pan. Cut the meat against its grain into 1-inch-thick slices. With two forks, shred the meat. Mix 1 cup of the reduced pomegranate juices into the meat and keep warm.

Warm the pitas in the oven for about 4 minutes.

Add the remaining pomegranate juices to the onions in the Dutch oven.

Serve piles of pulled meat on warm pitas and top with the onions and half of the tahini sauce. Scatter the pomegranate seeds and mint over the top. Serve the remaining tahini sauce on the side.

WARM TAHINI GRAIN BOWLS

V   DF   GF   FF   SERVES 4

What is it about tahini and bowls? They're everywhere! I think it's because both bowls and tahini shout out healthy, delicious, and effortless. You can use this recipe as a template, mixing any vegetable you have with any grain and any of the savory sauces from chapter 2.

3 cups cut vegetables, such as broccoli florets, carrots, red onion, or kale

Coarse sea salt and freshly ground black pepper

3 cups warm cooked brown rice or other whole grain

¾ cup sauerkraut or kimchi

1 cup bean sprouts

4 breakfast radishes or 1 watermelon radish, thinly sliced

¾ cup tahini dressing or sauce of choice (pages 34–61)

Large handful microgreens

2 tablespoons toasted sesame seeds

Put the vegetables in a single layer in a steaming basket and set over boiling water. Steam until the carrots are fork-tender, about 8 minutes. (Alternatively, turn the oven to 350°F. Set a cooling rack on a rimmed sheet pan and add water to the pan so that it covers the bottom but doesn't touch the bottom of the rack. Arrange the vegetables in a single layer on the rack and cover the whole pan with aluminum foil. Put in the oven and steam until the carrots are tender, about 12 minutes.) Season vegetables with salt and pepper, to taste.

Divide the steamed vegetables among four bowls and toss each with ¾ cup of the rice. Top with small mounds of sauerkraut, bean sprouts, and radish. Drizzle the tahini dressing over all. Top with the microgreens and a scattering of the sesame seeds.

LOADED TAHINI SWEET POTATOES

V   DF   GF   FF   SERVES 4

Creamy roasted sweet potatoes are drenched with a rich tahini sauce, with little bright bits of fresh tomato. One pan! Vegan! Gorgeous colors! Such an easy dinner! Hardly any cleanup! Works for me.

1 leek, trimmed, halved lengthwise, and thinly sliced (white and pale green parts)

1 (15-ounce) can chickpeas, rinsed and drained

2 tablespoons extra-virgin olive oil, divided

1 garlic clove, minced with coarse sea salt (see page 18)

1 teaspoon ground coriander

½ teaspoon ground cumin

½ teaspoon smoked paprika

Pinch ground cinnamon

Fine sea salt and freshly ground black pepper, to taste

4 medium sweet potatoes, halved lengthwise

1 bunch lacinato kale, coarsely chopped

1 cup Orange-Rosemary Tahini Sauce (page 34) or Sweet and Sour Tahini Dressing (page 46)

12 cherry tomatoes, quartered

¼ cup chopped fresh flat-leaf parsley

Hot sauce, to taste

Turn the oven to 400°F.

Toss the leek and chickpeas with 1 tablespoon of the olive oil on a rimmed sheet pan. Add the garlic, coriander, cumin, paprika, cinnamon, salt, and pepper and toss to coat everything evenly. Push the leek and chickpea mixture to the edges of the sheet pan.

Rub the cut surfaces of the sweet potatoes with the remaining 1 tablespoon of olive oil and season with salt and pepper. Put the sweet potatoes, cut-side down, in the center of the sheet pan. Bake until the potatoes are fork-tender, about 45 minutes.

While the potatoes are baking, boil the kale in a good amount of salted water until tender, about 12 minutes.

When the potatoes are tender, put two halves on each plate and flatten them with the back of a large fork. Transfer the kale to the sheet pan and toss with the chickpeas and leeks. Drizzle some of the tahini sauce over the potatoes and pile the veggies on top. Top with more tahini sauce and the tomatoes, parsley, and hot sauce.

TAHINI CHICKEN SCHNITZEL

DF **FF** SERVES 4

Who doesn't love fried chicken? For me, American fried chicken is surpassed only by Israeli chicken schnitzel, which in Israel is eaten every which way. Here we use tahini vinaigrette instead of a traditional egg wash and the outcome is a pretty sophisticated Schnitz.

2 cups Creamy Tahini Vinaigrette (page 42)

1 teaspoon ground cumin

½ teaspoon harissa seasoning or other dried hot pepper seasoning, divided

4 (8-ounce) boneless, skinless chicken breast halves

¾ cup panko bread crumbs or cornmeal

¾ cup all-purpose flour

1 tablespoon coarse sea salt

Mild vegetable oil, such as grapeseed, for frying

2 tablespoons chopped fresh herbs, such as flat-leaf parsley, dill, or thyme (optional)

Mix the tahini vinaigrette, cumin, and ¼ teaspoon of the harissa in a 2-cup liquid measuring cup (one with a handle and a spout). Pour half of vinaigrette mixture into a gallon-size zip-top plastic bag and set the rest aside.

Flatten the chicken breast halves by pushing down on the thicker parts with the flat of your palm, until each piece of chicken is no more than 1 inch thick at its thickest part. Try to make the thickness the same for each piece to keep the frying time consistent. Put the chicken in the bag with the vinaigrette mixture. Seal the bag, leaving an inch open at the corner, and squeeze the empty parts to force out any air. Zip it fully closed. Massage the bag to disperse the liquid all around the chicken and put in the refrigerator for at least 1 hour; longer (up to 24 hours) is better.

About 30 minutes before you're ready to serve, mix the breadcrumbs and all-purpose flour, salt, and remaining ¼ teaspoon of harissa on a plate.

Set a wire rack on a rimmed sheet pan or on a sheet of aluminum foil beside your flour plate. Designating one hand for only the dry flouring and one hand for only the wet chicken, use the "wet" hand to lift one piece of chicken from the marinade, allow any excess to drip back into the bag, and put the chicken in the flour.

recipe continues ▷

With your "dry" hand, flip the flour all around the edges of the chicken. Without touching the wet parts, use the same hand to flip the chicken over. Keep flipping until the chicken is well coated. With the same dry hand, lift the chicken and shake it gently to remove any loose flour, then transfer it to the prepared rack. Repeat this process with the rest of the chicken pieces, remembering to use your designated hands to prevent battering your fingers.

Put a large skillet over medium-high heat and fill with 1 inch of oil. Warm until an instant-read thermometer registers 355°F, about 5 minutes. (If you don't have a thermometer, you can test the temperature by sticking the end of a wooden spoon into the middle of the oil. If bubbles form within a few seconds, it's up to temp.) Turn the heat down to medium-low. Set a clean wire rack over another sheet pan or sheet of foil next to the stove.

Gently slip the breaded chicken into the hot oil, being careful not to splash. Fry until golden brown on the bottom side, about 3 minutes. (If it's still not brown at 5 minutes, turn up the heat a little.) Flip the chicken pieces over and fry on the other side until browned, about 3 minutes more. Be patient when frying. Rushing will make the crust too dark and hard. We're going for a lightly golden and delicately crisp crust.

Drain the chicken on the clean rack for a few seconds, then transfer to a serving platter. Drizzle some of the reserved vinaigrette mixture over the chicken and serve the rest on the side. Scatter the herbs (if using) over the top and serve right away.

SHEET PAN STIR-FRY

with Sweet Soy Tahini

VEG   DF   FF   SERVES 4

Stir-fries are fast, but they take all your attention while they're on the fire. Look away and they can scorch. Throwing the pan in a hot oven takes away all the stress. It takes about 20 minutes, but while it's cooking, you can be getting something else done.

Cooking spray, for greasing

1 pound protein, such as boneless, skinless chicken, extra-firm tofu, seitan, or beef tenderloin, cut into 1-inch chunks

2 carrots, cut into ½-inch-thick pieces

2 celery stalks, cut into ¼-inch-thick pieces

1 bell pepper (any color), seeded and cut into ½-inch pieces

1 head broccoli

3 tablespoons soy sauce, divided

2 tablespoons honey, divided

1 tablespoon toasted sesame oil

1 tablespoon grated fresh ginger, divided

1 cup Roasted Garlic Tahini Sauce (page 38)

1 teaspoon sriracha

1 cup snow peas

2 scallions, sliced (green and white parts)

1 tablespoon sesame seeds

Turn the oven to 425°F. Grease a rimmed sheet pan with cooking spray.

Toss the protein, carrots, celery, bell pepper, and broccoli on the prepared sheet pan with 2 tablespoons of the soy sauce, 1 tablespoon of the honey, the sesame oil, and ½ tablespoon of the ginger. Bake until the protein is no longer raw looking, about 12 minutes.

Meanwhile, mix the tahini sauce, remaining 1 tablespoon of soy sauce, 1 tablespoon of honey, and ½ tablespoon of ginger in a small bowl until smooth. Stir in the sriracha and set aside.

Add the snow peas, scallions, and sesame seeds to the sheet pan. Toss quickly and return to the oven for 5 more minutes.

Toss the roasted protein and vegetables with the tahini mixture and serve.

Tip: If you have some Tahini Stir-Fry Sauce (page 41) in the fridge, you can substitute that for the Roasted Garlic Tahini Sauce.

STUFFED EGGPLANT

with Tahini Drizzle

VEG   SERVES 4

These loaded eggplants are the perfect vegetarian dinner party entrée. They can be assembled a day ahead and baked once guests arrive.

4 small eggplants
3 tablespoons extra-virgin olive oil, divided
1 small onion, chopped
2 garlic cloves, chopped
Fine sea salt and freshly ground black pepper, to taste
1 (15-ounce) can cannellini beans, rinsed and drained
1 (14.5-ounce) can diced tomatoes, drained
2 cups Warm Spinach and Feta Tahini (page 89) or Roasted Carrot Tahini with Smoked Paprika (page 85)
Cooking spray
2 tablespoons freshly grated Parmesan cheese
2 tablespoons panko bread crumbs
1 cup Roasted Garlic Tahini Sauce (page 38) or Sweet and Sour Tahini Dressing (page 46)
¼ cup chopped fresh flat-leaf parsley or cilantro

Cut out a narrow wedge down the length of each eggplant and scrape out the interior flesh with a spoon, leaving enough to ensure that the remaining eggplant shell is sturdy. Chop the flesh you removed.

Heat 1 tablespoon of the olive oil in a large skillet over medium heat. Add the onion and chopped eggplant and sauté, chopping and turning with a spatula, until tender, about 8 minutes. Add the garlic, salt, and pepper and cook for another 30 seconds. Stir in the beans and tomatoes and cook until heated through. Scrape the eggplant mixture into a bowl and stir in the Spinach or Carrot Tahini. Wipe out the skillet.

Turn the oven to 375°F. Grease a 9 × 13-inch baking dish with cooking spray.

Season the eggplant shells with salt and pepper. Set the skillet over medium-high heat. Add the remaining 2 tablespoons of olive oil and the eggplants, cut-side down. Cook until the eggplants brown, about 5 minutes. Flip them and brown the other side, about 4 minutes more. Transfer the eggplants, cut-side up, to the prepared baking dish. Load the eggplant shells with the eggplant-tahini filling.

Mix the Parmesan and panko in a small bowl and sprinkle over the top of the eggplants. Bake until the eggplants are fork-tender, about 30 minutes.

Transfer the eggplants to a serving platter and drizzle the tahini sauce over the top. Sprinkle with the herb.

Tip: The Spinach and Feta Tahini goes best with the Roasted Garlic Tahini and parsley. The Smoked Paprika and Carrot Tahini pairs best with the Sweet and Sour Tahini and cilantro.

ROASTED TAHINI CAULIFLOWER

with Pistachios

V   DF   GF   P   SERVES 4

Through his two restaurants, Saba and Safta, Alon Shaya is a voice for Israeli cuisine in the States. He does a roasted cauliflower that was Shelby's and my favorite dish when we first ate at his restaurant. We've used it as inspiration for this dish so you can cook it as often as you like.

Cooking spray, for greasing
¼ cup premium tahini paste
1 garlic clove, minced with coarse sea salt (see page 18), divided
¼ cup freshly squeezed lemon juice
2 tablespoons extra-virgin olive oil
½ teaspoon hot sauce
½ teaspoon ground cardamom
½ teaspoon fine sea salt
¼ teaspoon freshly ground black pepper
1 large cauliflower head, leaves removed, stem cut flat
3 tablespoons finely chopped pistachio nuts
3 tablespoons minced fresh flat-leaf parsley

Turn the oven to 375°F. Grease a cast-iron skillet (or a pie pan or sheet pan) with cooking spray.

Mix the tahini, half of the garlic, the lemon juice, olive oil, hot sauce, cardamom, salt, and pepper in a small bowl.

Brush all but a couple of tablespoons of the tahini mixture all over the cauliflower with a pastry brush. It's easiest to do this by holding the cauliflower upside down in one hand and brushing the underside. Then invert onto the prepared pan and finish coating the top and sides. Roast until tender, about 1 hour.

While the cauliflower roasts, mix the pistachios, remaining garlic, and parsley in a small bowl.

Remove the cauliflower from the oven and brush the reserved tahini mixture over the top. Sprinkle the pistachio-parsley mixture over the top and return to the oven until the nuts are toasted, about 10 minutes.

Carve in wedges to serve.

COLD SESAME CHICKEN

DF **FF** SERVES 6

I know boiling chicken is unusual. I'd never done it until we tried this, but slowly simmering chicken with lots of aromatics flavors the meat through and through and keeps it incredibly moist. It's not going to get crispy like roasted chicken. The meat comes out soft and succulent, which is what makes it so good served cold (or warm or room temperature).

1 tablespoon five-spice powder

1 teaspoon ground fennel seed

1 teaspoon ground ginger

1 teaspoon garlic powder

1 teaspoon fine sea salt

3 pounds bone-in, skin-on chicken parts or 1 (3½- to 4-pound) whole chicken, split in half

2 tablespoons mild vegetable oil, such as grapeseed

1 bunch scallions, coarsely chopped (green and white parts)

1 (2-inch) piece fresh ginger, sliced

2 star anise pods

1 (2-inch) piece fresh turmeric, sliced, or 1 tablespoon ground turmeric

1 small dried or fresh red chile

Mix the five-spice powder, fennel, ground ginger, garlic powder, and salt in a small bowl. Rub it all over the chicken. Set aside for about 30 minutes or refrigerate for several hours.

Heat the oil in a Dutch oven over medium-high heat. Add the chicken and lightly brown each side, about 3 minutes per side. Don't let it get too dark; it should be golden brown.

Add just enough water to cover the chicken. Bring to a boil, then immediately turn the heat down to very low, so the water barely simmers. Stir in the scallions, fresh ginger, star anise, turmeric, and chile. Cover and cook as gently as possible until the chicken is just fork-tender, about 45 minutes. Transfer the chicken to a rimmed sheet pan to cool.

While the chicken is cooling, raise the heat to high under the pot of broth and boil until it is reduced by about half, about 10 minutes. Every now and then, spoon some of the boiling broth over the chicken while it cools.

- **1 garlic clove, minced with coarse sea salt (see page 18)**
- **½ cup premium tahini paste**
- **3 tablespoons soy sauce**
- **3 tablespoons silan date syrup**
- **1 teaspoon hot sauce**
- **½ cup chopped fresh cilantro**
- **1 tablespoon toasted sesame seeds**
- **12–15 roasted peanuts or other nuts, chopped**

Pour ½ cup of the reduced broth into a medium bowl. Mix in the minced garlic, tahini, soy sauce, date syrup, and hot sauce.

Arrange the chicken on a platter in a single layer. Brush with a thick layer of the tahini glaze. Scatter the cilantro, sesame seeds, and peanuts over the top and drizzle on the rest of the tahini glaze.

ADEENA SUSSMAN'S SKILLET CHICKEN

with Date Syrup, Sumac, and Tahini

DF **GF** P SERVES 4

Our friend Adeena Sussman is an American Israeli whose cooking style reflects her chosen home's culture: "complex but not complicated." Her cookbook *Sababa* was published when we were finishing up this manuscript. The word *sababa* means "awesome," exactly how I'd describe this chicken dish. Her friendship and reverence for tahini are hugely inspiring to my sisters and me.

For the sauce
- ½ cup premium tahini paste
- ½ cup silan date syrup
- ¼ cup low-sodium chicken broth
- 4 garlic cloves, minced
- 1 tablespoon dried sumac
- 1 teaspoon fine sea salt
- ½ teaspoon freshly ground black pepper

For the chicken
- 4 (6-ounce) bone-in, skin-on chicken thighs, trimmed of excess fat
- Fine sea salt and freshly ground black pepper, to taste
- 2 tablespoons extra-virgin olive oil, divided

Turn the oven to 400°F.

To make the sauce: Whisk the tahini, date syrup, chicken broth, garlic, sumac, salt, and pepper in a small bowl until combined. The sauce should be thick but pourable. Add a few tablespoons of water if you need to. Set it aside.

To make the chicken: Generously season the chicken on both sides with salt and pepper. Don't skimp! This is your chance to build flavor.

Heat 1 tablespoon of the olive oil in a heavy skillet over medium-high heat. Add the chicken, skin-side down, and cook without moving it for 5 minutes, or until the skin is golden and some of the fat has rendered. Flip the chicken and cook the other side until brown, about 3 minutes. Transfer the chicken to a plate.

Drain and discard all but 2 tablespoons of the fat from the pan, then add the onions and garlic and cook, stirring, until the onions are golden and the garlic begins to soften, 8 to 9 minutes. Return the chicken to the pan, pour the sauce on top, and transfer the skillet to the oven.

2 medium onions (about 1 pound), very thinly sliced

20 garlic cloves, pierced with the tip of a small paring knife

¼ cup low-sodium chicken broth

Chopped fresh cilantro or flat-leaf parsley, for garnish

Dried sumac, for sprinkling

Bake until the chicken is cooked through, the skin is caramelized, and the garlic cloves are roasted and golden, about 20 minutes. Transfer the chicken to a plate and keep warm.

Using a heavy pot holder, transfer the hot skillet to a burner. Stir the broth into the onions in the pan and bring to a boil over medium-high heat, then reduce the heat to medium and cook, stirring, until the mixture becomes saucy. Season with salt and pepper.

Spoon some of the onion sauce on four plates, top each pool of sauce with a piece of chicken, then spoon the rest of the sauce over the chicken. Garnish with the cilantro and sumac and serve.

CHAPTER 7

SWEETS

CARDAMOM HALVAH

with Pistachios

V   DF   **GF**   MAKES ABOUT 1 POUND

I know that making candy from scratch sounds over-the-top—images of scalding sugar syrup and chocolate fingerprints on counters and cabinets—but I've tried it, and though I'm far from a master, I can whip up a batch of halvah pretty easily. The trick to halvah is getting the texture right. If your sugar syrup is too hot, it turns into sand. If it's not hot enough, it becomes too creamy, like mall fudge. I can't tell you this recipe is foolproof. If you beat it too much or heat it too little, your result won't be optimal, but it will still be delicious. Tahini, cardamom, lemon, and pistachio? You can't screw up a flavor combination like that.

Cooking spray, for greasing

1 (11-ounce) jar premium tahini paste (about 1½ cups)

1 cup finely chopped pistachios

1 vanilla bean

2 cups granulated sugar

1½ teaspoons ground cardamom

¾ teaspoon fine sea salt

½ cup brewed chai or other spiced tea

Grease an 8- or 9-inch-square baking pan with cooking spray and line the bottom with parchment paper. Have another piece of parchment ready to cover the top.

In a stand mixer fitted with the paddle attachment, combine the tahini and pistachios and mix until just incorporated. Turn off the mixer.

Slit the vanilla bean in half lengthwise and scrape the seeds from the interior with a small knife. Mix the vanilla seeds, sugar, cardamom, salt, and chai in a medium saucepan over medium heat, stirring until the sugar dissolves. Bring the chai mixture to a boil, without stirring, until the syrup is thick and registers 240°F to 242°F on an instant-read thermometer, about 2 minutes.

Immediately turn the stand mixer to medium-low speed and drizzle the hot syrup into the tahini mixture. Mix just enough for the batter to begin to pull away from the sides of the bowl but no longer, about 30 seconds.

Quickly pour and scrape the batter into the prepared pan and press the top flat with the parchment. Cool completely before cutting into squares with a serrated knife.

Store tightly wrapped at room temperature for up to 1 week.

SEEDY HALVAH

V   DF   GF   FF   MAKES ABOUT 1 POUND

This halvah is just as easy as the previous recipe. It is mildly flavored with ginger and vanilla, and beautifully golden from turmeric and saffron. Loading it up with lots of sesame seeds gives it a little bit of the character of classic hard sesame candies (see page 201).

Cooking spray, for greasing

1 (11-ounce) jar premium tahini paste (about 1½ cups)

2½ cups sesame seeds (a mix of toasted, white, and black)

1 vanilla bean

2 cups granulated sugar

1½ teaspoons ground turmeric

½ teaspoon saffron threads

¾ teaspoon fine sea salt

½ cup brewed ginger tea

Grease an 8- or 9-inch square baking pan with cooking spray and line the bottom with parchment paper. Have another piece of parchment ready to cover the top.

In a stand mixer fitted with the paddle attachment, combine the tahini and sesame seeds and mix until just incorporated. Turn off the mixer.

Slit the vanilla bean in half lengthwise and scrape the seeds from the interior with a small knife. Mix the vanilla seeds, sugar, turmeric, saffron, salt, and tea in a medium saucepan over medium heat, stirring until the sugar dissolves. Bring the ginger tea mixture to a boil, without stirring, until the syrup is thick and registers 240°F to 242°F on an instant-read thermometer, about 2 minutes.

Immediately turn the stand mixer to medium-low speed and drizzle the hot syrup into the tahini mixture. Mix just enough for the batter to begin to pull away from the sides of the bowl but no longer, about 30 seconds.

Quickly pour and scrape the batter into the prepared pan and press the top flat with the parchment. Cool completely before cutting into squares with a serrated knife.

Store tightly wrapped at room temperature for up to 1 week.

TAHINI PEANUT CHEWS

V   DF   GF   FF   MAKES 36 CANDIES

Our mom grew up in and around Philly, so for her Goldenberg's Peanut Chews was the epitome of candy bars. Dipped in dark chocolate and with a crunchy, chewy molasses center, it was what a Snickers would want to be when it grew up. Sadly, the company got bought and they are hard to come by now. These easy-to-make bite-size candies are our attempt to bring them back.

Cooking spray, for greasing

1 cup lightly salted dry-roasted peanuts

½ cup roasted hazelnuts, almonds, or cashews, coarsely chopped

6 tablespoons premium tahini paste

¼ cup silan date syrup

¼ cup malt syrup

½ teaspoon vanilla extract

⅛ teaspoon fine sea salt

1 pound semisweet chocolate, finely chopped

⅓ cup white sesame seeds

Grease an 8-inch-square baking dish with cooking spray and line the bottom with parchment paper or aluminum foil.

Pulse the peanuts and hazelnuts in a food processor about 5 times, until uniformly but chunkily chopped. Add the tahini, date syrup, malt syrup, vanilla, and salt and pulse about 4 times, until everything sticks together but still has a chunky, nutty texture.

Pack the tahini mixture in an even layer in the prepared baking dish, cover with another sheet of parchment, and refrigerate until firm, at least 2 hours.

Cut the chilled tahini mixture into 36 squares and put the baking dish in the freezer while you melt the chocolate.

Put half of the chocolate in a microwave-safe bowl. Cover loosely and microwave on full power until melted, 2 to 3 minutes. Uncover and whisk the chocolate until smooth. (Alternatively, put the chocolate in a tempered glass or stainless steel bowl and set it over a pot of simmering water; stir until the chocolate is smooth.) Whisk the rest of the chopped chocolate into the melted chocolate in three additions, waiting until each addition is fully incorporated before adding the next.

Set a wire rack in a rimmed sheet pan lined with parchment or foil. Remove the squares from the freezer. One at a time, coat them in the melted chocolate, turning them over carefully with two forks until completely coated. Transfer to the wire rack with the forks, then sprinkle the top with sesame seeds. Allow the chews to cool at room temperature until the chocolate is no longer shiny, about 1 hour, then refrigerate until the chocolate is solid.

Store in a closed container in the refrigerator for up to 2 weeks or in the freezer for up to 3 months.

HALVAH DATE TRUFFLES

V   DF   GF   FF   P   MAKES ABOUT 2 DOZEN TRUFFLES

Chocolate truffles are the chocolate chip cookie of confection—so foolproof and effortless and delicious that you don't need too much candy-making skill to find success. This recipe takes advantage of tahini's tendency to thicken when it's combined with a small amount of moisture—in this case a combo of orange juice, date syrup, and chocolate—turning it instantly into a creamy bite-size sweet.

6 Medjool dates, pitted and finely chopped

¼ cup freshly squeezed orange juice

¼ cup silan date syrup

3 tablespoons premium tahini paste

4 ounces dark chocolate, finely chopped

½ cup toasted sesame seeds

Put the dates, orange juice, date syrup, and tahini in a small saucepan and bring to a boil over medium heat, stirring the whole time. Remove the pan from the heat and stir in the chocolate until it's melted. Cool to room temperature, then refrigerate until firm, about 1 hour.

Scoop small rounds, about 2 teaspoons each, and roll into rough balls in the sesame seeds.

Store in a closed container in the refrigerator for up to 2 weeks.

SESAME TAHINI CANDY

V   DF   GF   FF   MAKES ABOUT 4 DOZEN CANDIES

These utterly professional-looking hard candies come together in less than 2 minutes and are stiff competition to Joyva Sesame Crunch candies that were standard Passover fare at our grandparents' apartment. They don't require a candy thermometer, and they can be stored at room temperature for weeks.

Cooking spray, for greasing
1 cup white sesame seeds
¼ cup granulated sugar
¼ cup silan date syrup
¼ teaspoon fine sea salt
2 tablespoons premium tahini paste

Grease a sheet pan with cooking spray.

Mix the sesame seeds, sugar, date syrup, and salt in a medium saucepan over medium heat. Cook, stirring frequently to keep the mixture from scorching, until the sugar mixture is an aromatic, richly browned syrup that coats the bottom of the pan, about 4 minutes. Remove the pan from the heat and stir in the tahini. Return to medium heat and cook until the mixture pulls away from the sides of the pan, about 1 minute, stirring hard the whole time. Immediately scrape the candy mixture into the prepared pan and flatten to a rough ¼-inch-thick rectangle with a silicone spatula. Let cool for about 3 minutes.

Using a wide spatula, slide the candy rectangle onto a cutting board while it's still warm and pliable. Cut into 1-inch squares. Eat right away or wait until it hardens, about 1 hour.

Store in a tightly closed container at room temperature for up to 1 month.

GIANT CHOCOLATE JUMBLES

VEG   GF   FF   MAKES 2 DOZEN LARGE COOKIES

These whopper chocolate oatmeal cookies have no flour and therefore no gluten. They are so easy to mix up, and they will stay fresh in a cookie jar for weeks. To store them for longer, wrap them individually in plastic and freeze them. Whenever you're in the mood, grab one, pop it in the microwave for 20 seconds, and enjoy a freshly baked cookie.

½ cup (1 stick) unsalted butter, at room temperature

1 (12-ounce) jar chocolate tahini (about 1½ cups)

1 cup packed dark brown sugar

½ teaspoon ground cinnamon

½ teaspoon fine sea salt

3 large eggs

1 tablespoon baking soda

1 tablespoon vanilla extract

¼ teaspoon almond extract

5 cups old-fashioned oats

1½ cups semisweet chocolate chips

1½ cups dried sour cherries or raisins

Set two oven racks near the center of the oven. Turn the oven to 350°F. Line two sheet pans with parchment paper or silicone baking mats.

Mix the butter, chocolate tahini, brown sugar, cinnamon, and salt in a large bowl with a wooden spoon until smooth. Beat in the eggs. Mix the baking soda, vanilla, and almond extract in a small bowl until smooth, then mix into the tahini mixture. Add the oats, chocolate chips, and cherries, mixing just enough to moisten them.

Scoop the batter with a ¼-cup measure and arrange as mounds on the prepared pans, about 2½ inches apart. You should be able to fit six cookies per sheet pan. Wet your hands and flatten the mounds so that each is about ½ inch thick.

Bake until set, about 15 minutes, switching the pans between racks halfway through. Cool the cookies on the pans for 5 minutes, then transfer them to wire racks to cool completely. When the pans are at room temperature again, form the remaining batter into cookies and bake in the same way.

Store in a closed container at room temperature for up to 2 weeks.

TAHINI SUGAR COOKIES

VEG   FF   MAKES 30 COOKIES

Like a classic peanut butter cookie crossed with shortbread, these very plain and wonderfully rich biscuits are the perfect accompaniment to a cup of coffee or tea.

- 6 tablespoons (¾ stick) unsalted butter, at room temperature
- ½ cup premium tahini paste
- ½ cup granulated sugar
- ½ cup packed light brown sugar
- ¼ teaspoon fine sea salt
- 1 large egg
- 1 teaspoon vanilla extract
- 1¼ cups all-purpose flour
- ½ teaspoon baking soda
- 2 tablespoons raw sugar, such as demerara or turbinado, and/or sesame seeds (optional)

Set two oven racks near the center of the oven. Turn the oven to 350°F. Line two sheet pans with parchment paper or silicone baking mats.

Beat the butter, tahini, granulated sugar, brown sugar, and salt in a large bowl with a wooden spoon until just combined. Mix in the egg and vanilla.

Mix the flour and baking soda in a small bowl, then stir the flour mixture into the batter until it is no longer visible.

Scoop the batter with a 1-tablespoon measure and arrange as mounds on the prepared pans, about 1½ inches apart. You should be able to fit 10 cookies per sheet. Wet your hands and flatten the mounds so that each is about ⅜ inch thick. Sprinkle the tops with the raw sugar or sesame seeds (if using).

Bake until the bottoms are lightly browned, about 10 minutes, switching the pans between racks halfway through. Cool the cookies on the pans for 5 minutes, then transfer them to wire racks to cool completely. When the pans are at room temperature again, form the remaining batter into cookies and bake in the same way.

Store in a closed container at room temperature for up to 4 days or freeze for up to 1 month.

Tahini Sugar Cookie Sandwiches: For a real treat of a variation, sandwich chocolate tahini or ice cream between two of these cookies.

TEHINA REGINA COOKIES

VEG   DF   MAKES ABOUT 40 COOKIES

The origin of regina cookies, golden pillows pavéed with a rash of sesame seeds, is Sicilian. This recipe ups the ante of sesame (and greatly reduces the saturated fat) by substituting tahini for the traditional butter.

½ cup premium tahini paste

1 cup granulated sugar

3 large eggs

1½ teaspoons vanilla extract

⅛ teaspoon almond extract

2¼ cups all-purpose flour

2½ teaspoons baking powder

½ teaspoon fine sea salt

¼ teaspoon ground cardamom

1 cup white sesame seeds

Mix the tahini and sugar in a large bowl until well combined. Beat in the eggs, vanilla, and almond extract until the mixture is smooth.

Mix the flour, baking powder, salt, and cardamom in a medium bowl, then stir the flour mixture into the batter just until there are no visible dry spots. The dough will be very stiff. Wrap it in plastic and refrigerate for at least 1 hour or as long as 24 hours.

Set two oven racks near the center of the oven. Turn the oven to 350°F. Line two sheet pans with parchment paper or silicone baking mats.

Put the sesame seeds in wide bowl. Scoop the dough with a 1-tablespoon measure and arrange as mounds on a big sheet of aluminum foil, plastic wrap, or parchment. Wet your hands and roll the mounds into egg-shaped ovals. As each one is made, coat all over with sesame seeds and place on the prepared pans, about 1 inch apart. You will get 13 to 14 cookies per pan.

Bake until golden brown, about 10 minutes. Cool the cookies for 2 minutes on the pans, then transfer them to wire racks to cool completely. When the pans are at room temperature again, form the remaining batter into cookies and bake in the same way.

Store in a closed container at room temperature for up to 2 weeks.

TAHINI S'MORES MARSHMALLOWS

FF   MAKES 36 EXTRA-LARGE MARSHMALLOWS

This recipe is inspired by the tahini-laced marshmallows developed by Sheri Silver for the Nosher. Marshmallows are nothing but gelatin, cooked and sweetened by hot sugar syrup, that is inflated to twenty times its volume by an electric mixer. They are incredibly easy and fun to make—a great cooking project for seven- to ten-year-olds.

Cooking spray, for greasing

⅔ cup graham cracker crumbs

⅓ cup confectioners' sugar

3 (¼-ounce) packets unflavored gelatin

1 cup cold water, divided

1 cup light corn syrup

1½ cups granulated sugar

¼ teaspoon fine sea salt

1 teaspoon vanilla extract

½ cup premium tahini paste

4 ounces milk or dark chocolate, finely chopped and melted

Lightly grease an 8- or 9-inch-square baking pan with cooking spray.

Combine the graham cracker crumbs and confectioners' sugar in a small bowl. Sprinkle half of the mixture into the prepared pan, tilting it to evenly coat the bottom.

Combine the gelatin and ½ cup of the water in a stand mixer fitted with the whisk attachment; let it sit.

Combine the remaining ½ cup of water, corn syrup, granulated sugar, and salt in a small, heavy saucepan. Cover and cook over medium-high heat for 3 minutes. Uncover and continue cooking until the syrup registers 240°F on an instant-read thermometer. Start measuring after about 5 minutes of cooking. Immediately remove the pan from the heat. It's important that the sugar be right at 240°F. If it's too cold, the marshmallows won't set. If it gets too hot, the marshmallows will be crunchy instead of chewy.

Immediately turn the stand mixture to low speed and drizzle the hot syrup into the gelatin mixture. Once all of the syrup has been added, gradually turn up the speed to high. After 5 minutes, add the vanilla. Continue to beat until the mixture is thick and white and barely warm, about 5 minutes more.

recipe continues ▷

Grease a silicone spatula with cooking spray and stir in the tahini, leaving it a little streaky.

Grease the spatula again and use it to scrape the marshmallow mixture into the prepared pan. Drizzle the melted chocolate over the top and use the spatula to swirl the chocolate through the marshmallow. Don't mix it too much; the chocolate should be swirly, not fully mixed in.

Grease the spatula again and smooth the top, making sure the marshmallow gets all the way into the corners of the pan. If the spatula starts sticking to the marshmallow, use more cooking spray.

Scatter the rest of the sugar mixture on top and spread it evenly with your fingers. Set aside to dry for at least 6 hours or overnight.

Turn the marshmallow sheet out onto a large cutting board. Coat a knife with cooking spray and cut the marshmallows into 1½-inch squares. Roll the cut surface of the marshmallows with any sugar mixture that has fallen out of the pan onto the cutting board.

Store in a closed container at room temperature for up to 3 months.

NO-COOK CHOCOLATE TAHINI PUDDING

V   DF   **GF**   **FF**   SERVES 2

This is our rendition of the popular internet recipe for vegan instant pudding made with avocado in place of cream and egg. We make it even tastier and richer with tahini.

1 ripe avocado, halved and pitted

6 tablespoons chocolate tahini

2 tablespoons silan date syrup

1 teaspoon vanilla extract

Large pinch coarse sea salt

Chopped chocolate or nuts or crumbled halvah, for topping

Scrape the avocado into a food processor. Add the chocolate tahini, date syrup, vanilla, and salt and pulse until smooth, scraping the sides as needed.

Spoon into dessert dishes, cover, and refrigerate for at least 30 minutes to set. Serve topped with chopped chocolate.

TAHINI FLAN

VEG **GF** FF SERVES 4

Flan (baked custard with caramel sauce) is a treat for any and all ages—it's magical (sweetened milk made solid), delicious (nutty, sweet, creamy), and pretty nutritious for a dessert (milk, eggs, and tahini give it lots of protein). If you've never made flan before, some of the cooking techniques (caramelizing sugar and baking in a water bath) might be new. But nothing is really difficult, and the results are so comforting and elegant. When's the last time those two things ever went together? It will quickly become a go-to dessert.

For the caramel
¾ cup granulated sugar

For the custard
2 cups 2% milk
½ cup granulated sugar
3 large eggs
3 tablespoons premium tahini paste
½ teaspoon vanilla extract
⅛ teaspoon almond extract
4 tablespoons toasted sesame seeds

Turn the oven to 350°F. Put four (8-ounce) ramekins within easy reach.

To make the caramel: In a deep, heavy skillet, melt the sugar over medium-high heat to a golden caramel, stirring with a long-handled wooden spoon the whole time. At first the sugar won't do much, but then you'll notice that it gets sticky in spots. Keep stirring and it will soon become pretty lumpy. Keep going and soon the sugar will start to brown and become liquid, with lumps floating in it. You may have to push on the lumps to break them up, but be careful. If the hot syrup splashes on your skin, it will give you a nasty burn.

When the caramel is deep brown and all the lumps have melted, about 4 minutes, carefully pour it into the ramekins, filling each one just enough to coat the bottom by about ¼ inch. Set the ramekins in a baking pan that is large enough to hold them without touching.

To make the custard: Whisk the milk and sugar in a small saucepan over medium heat. Cook, stirring occasionally, until bubbles form around the edge of the pan, about 5 minutes. Don't let it boil.

recipe continues ▷

Meanwhile, whisk the eggs, tahini, vanilla, and almond extract in a medium bowl. Slowly pour the heated milk into the egg mixture, whisking the whole time, until combined. Pour the milk-egg mixture into the caramel-lined ramekins. Sprinkle 1 tablespoon of sesame seeds on top of each one. Pour warm water into the baking pan, enough to come halfway up the sides of the ramekins.

Bake until a knife inserted in the center of one of the custards comes out with just a speck of custard clinging to it, about 30 minutes.

Cool the whole baking pan with the custards in it on a wire rack to room temperature. Remove the ramekins from the baking pan, cover each with plastic wrap, and refrigerate for several hours, until thoroughly chilled. They can be stored in the refrigerator for up to 2 days before serving.

To serve, run a knife around the perimeter of each custard and cover with a dessert plate. Invert and shake lightly to release the custard. When the custard drops from the ramekin, lift off the ramekin, allowing the caramel sauce to run over the top of the flan and down onto the plate.

HALVAH ICE CREAM

VEG   GF   FF   MAKES 1 QUART

Nothing is better than homemade ice cream, but mixing in nuggets of halvah is better than better. If you don't have an ice cream maker (or you just can't wait), check out the quick variation that uses commercial ice cream.

3 cups light cream, or 2 cups heavy cream plus 1 cup whole milk
¾ cup granulated sugar
⅔ cup premium tahini paste
1 teaspoon vanilla extract
½ teaspoon fine salt
4 ounces Seedy Halvah, (page 195), Cardamom Halvah (page 194), or store-bought halvah, crumbled in small pieces
Honey, for serving

Whisk the cream, sugar, tahini, vanilla, and salt in a large bowl until smooth.

Freeze in an ice cream maker following the manufacturer's instructions, then fold in the halvah. Transfer to a closed container and freeze for at least 2 hours, until firm.

Serve scoops drizzled with honey.

Store in a closed container in the freezer for up to 1 week.

Cheatin' Halvah Ice Cream: To make a quick version, soften 1 quart of premium vanilla ice cream at room temperature for 10 minutes. Give it a good stir to make it malleable, then add the halvah candy and stir to combine. Return to the freezer for about 30 minutes to firm up a little before scooping.

BOTANICA'S BUCKWHEAT TAHINI BROWNIES

VEG   GF   FF   SERVES 16

These healthy yet hearty and decadent brownies were created by Emily Fiffer and Heather Sperling, food mavens and owners of Botanica restaurant in Los Angeles. They were kind enough to give us the recipe for this book, and they go great with our halvah ice cream.

Cooking spray, for greasing
½ cup (1 stick) unsalted butter, thinly sliced
3 tablespoons cacao nibs
4 ounces 85% dark chocolate, finely chopped
¾ cup coconut palm sugar or other raw sugar
½ vanilla bean
4 large eggs
1 teaspoon fine sea salt
⅔ cup buckwheat flour
⅓ cup premium tahini paste, well mixed

Turn the oven to 350°F. Grease an 8-inch square baking pan with cooking spray and line the bottom with parchment paper or aluminum foil.

Stir the butter and cacao nibs in a medium saucepan over low heat until the butter just melts. Remove from the heat. Add the chocolate and stir until the chocolate is melted.

Slit the vanilla bean in half lengthwise and scrape the seeds from the interior with a small knife. Mix the vanilla seeds and sugar into the chocolate mixture. Beat in the eggs and salt. Add the flour and mix just enough to blend. Pour the batter into the prepared pan. Pour the tahini over the top, using a butter knife to swirl it through the batter.

Bake until the top is set, the cake is still soft in middle, and a skewer inserted in the center comes out slightly damp, about 15 minutes, rotating the pan halfway through. These brownies can go from "just right" to bone-dry in a flash, so when in doubt, pull them out! You can't go wrong with a soft middle.

Cool on a wire rack to room temperature, then refrigerate until firm before slicing. Store in a tightly closed container at room temperature for up to 3 days, or freeze individually wrapped for up to 1 month.

TAHINI OATMEAL RAISIN COOKIES

VEG GF FF MAKES 18 COOKIES

Every parent needs a healthy cookie recipe. This is Jackie's, and now it's yours. The brown sugar and the oats keep them super moist. You can use an electric mixer if you want, but I find it easier just to mix it up in a bowl with a wooden spoon (way less cleanup). Soaking the raisins in hot water makes them plump and squashy. Hard raisins in soft chewy cookies are such a turnoff.

1 cup raisins

¼ cup premium tahini paste

4 tablespoons (½ stick) unsalted butter, at room temperature

¾ cup light or dark brown sugar

1 teaspoon vanilla extract

½ teaspoon fine sea salt

1 large egg

¾ cup whole-wheat flour

½ teaspoon baking soda

½ teaspoon ground cinnamon

1½ cups old-fashioned oats

Set two oven racks near the center of the oven. Turn the oven to 375°F. Line two sheet pans with parchment paper or silicone baking mats.

Put the raisins in a small bowl and cover with boiling water; set aside.

Mix the tahini, butter, brown sugar, vanilla, and salt in a large bowl until everything is smooth and creamy. Beat in the egg.

Mix the flour, baking soda, and cinnamon in another bowl, then mix into the batter until just combined. Drain the raisins and stir them into the batter. Stir in the oats.

Scoop the batter with a 1-ounce cookie scoop or soup spoon onto the prepared pans, about 1½ inches apart. You should get nine per sheet. Wet your hands and flatten the cookies to a ½-inch thickness.

Bake until the edges are brown but the center still looks pale, about 10 minutes, switching the pans between racks halfway through. Cool the cookies on the pans for 5 minutes, then transfer them to a wire rack to cool completely.

Store in a closed container at room temperature for up to 5 days, or freeze for up to 1 month.

RACHELLA'S TAHINI CARROT CAKE

VEG **FF** SERVES 8

This recipe from Omri's mom, Rachella, is the one that woke me and my sisters to the power of tahini. The cake is super moist and rich. The tahini gives it a nutty aftertaste, and because the tahini reduces the amount of oil in the recipe, this cake never gets greasy the way many carrot cakes do.

For the batter

Cooking spray, for greasing
4 large eggs
1½ cups lightly packed light brown sugar
¾ cup mild vegetable oil, such as grapeseed
¾ cup premium tahini paste
1¼ cups whole-wheat pastry flour
1 tablespoon ground cinnamon
1 teaspoon ground allspice
1 teaspoon baking soda
½ teaspoon baking powder
½ teaspoon fine sea salt
7 medium carrots, peeled and shredded (about 2½ cups)
1½ cups chopped walnuts (optional)

Turn the oven to 350°F. Grease two (8-inch) round cake pans with cooking spray.

To make the batter: In a large bowl or in a stand mixer, beat the eggs and brown sugar until completely combined and thick. Beat in the oil, a bit at a time, then beat in the tahini.

Mix the flour, cinnamon, allspice, baking soda, baking powder, and salt in a separate bowl until combined. Add a third of the flour mixture to the tahini mixture, stirring to combine. Add half of the carrots and mix well. Add half of the remaining flour mixture, then the remaining carrots, and then the remaining flour mixture, stirring between each addition to combine. Stir in the walnuts (if using).

Divide the batter evenly between the prepared cake pans and bake on the middle rack of the oven until a skewer inserted in the center comes out clean, about 35 minutes. Cool in the pans for 15 minutes. Remove the cakes from the pans, then transfer them to wire racks to cool completely.

For the frosting

½ cup (1 stick) unsalted butter, at room temperature, cut into small pieces

1 (8-ounce) package cream cheese, at room temperature

½ cup premium tahini paste

2 cups confectioners' sugar

½ cup black and white sesame seeds

To make the frosting: While the cakes are baking, beat the butter, cream cheese, and tahini in a stand mixer (or large bowl) until smooth. Add the confectioners' sugar and mix until just smooth. If the frosting is too soft to spread, chill in the refrigerator for about 10 minutes.

Set one cake layer on a serving plate. Top with a third of the frosting and 2 tablespoons of the mixed sesame seeds. Add the next layer and frost the sides and top with the remaining frosting. Top with the remaining sesame seeds (it's fine if some fall down the sides). If the cake seems at all wobbly, refrigerate until the icing firms and the cake feels sturdy. Cut into wedges and serve.

CREAMY DAIRY-FREE TAHINI SORBET

VEG   DF   GF   FF   MAKES ABOUT 1 QUART

Technically this dessert is sorbet because it has no cream, but the richness of the coconut milk combined with tahini gives it the mouthfeel of premium ice cream.

1 (14-ounce) can full-fat coconut milk, well mixed

⅓ cup premium tahini paste

⅓ cup honey

¼ cup freshly squeezed orange juice

1½ teaspoons vanilla extract

⅛ teaspoon almond extract

Blend everything in a blender or a food processor until smooth, then pour into a shallow baking pan, such as a brownie pan or pie pan. Freeze until solid, at least 2 hours, or up to 2 days.

Cut into cubes with a sharp knife and purée in a food processor until smooth. Scoop and serve.

Store in a closed container in the freezer for up to 3 days.

DARK CHOCOLATE TAHINI BROWNIES

VEG   DF   GF   FF   MAKES 16 BROWNIES

I'm completely tolerant of gluten, but if you're not, these brownies are made with you in mind. They are extremely fudgy and moist—exactly what you want in brownies. The addition of tahini makes them almost as healthy as they are decadent.

Cooking spray, for greasing
1 (12-ounce) jar chocolate tahini (about 1½ cups)
⅓ cup coconut palm sugar or other raw sugar
1 tablespoon rice flour or coconut flour
¼ cup Dutch-process cocoa powder
½ teaspoon baking soda
¼ teaspoon fine sea salt
3 tablespoons honey or pure maple syrup
1 teaspoon vanilla extract
2 large eggs
¼ cup semisweet chocolate chips

Turn the oven to 350°F. Grease the inside of an 8- or 9-inch-square baking pan with cooking spray, then line the bottom with parchment paper. Spray the parchment with cooking spray.

Mix the tahini, sugar, flour, cocoa powder, baking soda, salt, honey, vanilla, eggs, and chocolate chips in a large bowl until everything is combined. Scrape the batter into the prepared pan, smoothing the top evenly. Bake until a skewer inserted in the center comes out with a few moist crumbs clinging to it, about 25 minutes.

Cool the brownies on a wire rack for 15 minutes, then cut into squares.

Store tightly wrapped at room temperature for up to 3 days, or freeze for up to 1 month.

ACKNOWLEDGMENTS

To the team at Agate for your collaborative and professional approach to publishing books. I feel so fortunate to be on your list of brilliant, diverse, and upstanding authors.

To Jillian Guyette and Lisa Russell for shouldering the art direction, styling, and photography of these dishes. These photographs convey tahini's brilliance thanks to you.

To Ana Sortun, Emily Fiffer and Heather Sperling, Jamie Vespa, and Adeena Sussman for sharing your recipes in these pages and supporting our vision for incorporating tahini into every course on our table.

Adeena, you've been an invaluable friend and ally in championing tahini.

To Mike Solomonov and Steve Cook for writing the foreword, for your partnership and friendship, and for welcoming our Soom family into yours at CookNSolo. We are so proud to be a part of your remarkable contributions to the world's culinary ethos.

To Andy. Your espousal of cooking and eating better with tahini was vital for the execution of this project. Thank you for sharing your wealth of culinary information and writing skills with me. I know I got more than I bargained for, but our time together writing this book and cooking these recipes has left an imprint on me that will last a lifetime.

To the Soom Crew for supporting our dream of making tahini a pantry staple in the American market. Your hard work and dedication inspire me daily. We're the luckiest to be able to learn and grow with you day in and day out.

To Omri and the *mishpucha*, and to our colleagues in Israel, Palestine, and Ethiopia and around the world who love and value tahini as much as we do.

To our mom and dad for setting the foundation on which we could build Soom Foods. Your examples of hard work, tzedakah (philanthropy), and living with values are the basis for why we are who we are. Thank you for making us share a bathroom and a computer.

To Shelby and Jackie. This book may be from my voice, but you two are so much a part of who I am that it is from all of us. Thank you for this incredible journey of entrepreneurship and self-discovery. I love, like, trust, and respect you both more than I can express.

To Darren. Since the day you bought a whole case of Soom right out of the trunk of my car on our second date, you've supported me more than I could have imagined. Thank you for creating a life, family, and home with me and for caring for all three whole-heartedly.

RESOURCES

Citrus squeezer: *Bellemain* | thebellemain.com
Citrus zester / channel knife: *OXO* | oxo.com
Citrus juices: *Santa Cruz* | santacruzorganic.com
Fine-tooth (rasp) grater: *Microplane* | us.microplane.com
Halvah: *Hebel & Co* | hebelco.com
Herbs and spices: *Burlap and Barrel* | burlapandbarrel.com
The Reluctant Trading Experiment | reluctantrading.com
Salts: *The Meadow* | themeadow.com
Tahini and date syrup: *Soom* | soomfoods.com

INDEX

ABOUT THE AUTHORS

Amy Zitelman is CEO and cofounder of Soom Foods, the leading purveyor of tahini and tahini products in the American market. Amy received her bachelor's degree in communication from the University of Delaware. After graduation, she spent time soaking up Israeli culture and teaching English in Israel. Upon her return to the states, she began working on bringing premium tahini to the American market with her sisters. Soom Foods was officially founded in 2013. Soom has been named the best tahini according to industry experts by *New York Magazine*'s "The Stategist" and has been featured in outlets like *New York Times*, *Food & Wine*, and *Bon Appetit*. In 2018, Amy was named to Forbes "30 under 30" in the Food and Beverage category.

Andrew Schloss is the author of twenty-four cookbooks, including *Mastering the Grill* (winner of a World Gourmand Award and a New York Times best seller) and *The Science of Good Food* (winner of an IACP Cookbook Award, a James Beard finalist, and nominated by Le Cordon Bleu Food Media Awards as Best Food Book in the World), both co-authored with David Joachim; *Fifty Ways to Cook Most Everything* (a main selection for Book of the Month's Home Style Club); *Homemade Soda*; *One-Pot Cakes*; *Fire It Up*, *The Art of the Slow Cooker*; Cooking Slow; and *Homemade Liqueurs and Infused Spirits*. His most recent book is a food science book for kids, *Amazing (Mostly) Edible Science*.